NOT MADE FOR
Quitting

BY DR. DICK HILLIS

BETHANY FELLOWSHIP, INC.
Minneapolis, Minn.

Bethany Fellowship, Inc.
6820 Auto Club Road
Minneapolis, Minnesota 55438
Printed in the United States of America

Contents

3

DEDICATED TO
John
Salpi
Jack
Margaret
David
Nancy
Stephen
Nan
Jennifer
Brian
and others like them with the spiritual steel
to carry on where we leave off.

Foreword

Here is a series of almost twenty brief biographical sketches. Some are well known ... some are not, but each one of the subjects has made a significant contribution to humanity.

The vital relationship between "doing" and "knowing" the will of God is brought into correct focus as the book catches the reflection of our own individual problems. The honest recording of problems, perplexities and weaknesses not only reveals God's faithfulness but makes possible a personal identification on the part of the reader.

The book brings a great challenge for young people, for underlying each of the sketches Dick Hillis indicates the motivation which eventuated in service.

Preface

Biographies of the great can either challenge or crush us. We are challenged by their commitment to Christ, their courage in conflict, their fearless fortitude and faith. But the mountains they have climbed are too high and the rivers they have crossed are too deep for us. They are God's tall men and we are His midgets.

This book will lead you into the secret places of some of the tall men. Some, but not many, mighty men are used of God. You will also discover the same secrets of His infinite care and direction in His little men. Little men with a big God . . . your God as well as theirs.

The same Lord who led them will lead you. It is usually the ordinary man who puts himself in the hands of a great Savior who sees extraordinary things done for God's glory.

Of the formulating of formulas there is no end. Therefore, this book does not attempt a doctrinal study on God's will and how to find it. It records the testimonies of men of the past and the present who have discovered His way and accomplished His will.

On purpose I have chosen men of diverse character and culture. I have written about the known and the unknown. Do not get disturbed if the key that unlocked Borden's life and led him in the way does not unlock yours.

The key you need may be found in the chapter of some man of whom you have never heard. Search on, for you have His promise . . .

"Seek and ye shall find."

CHAPTER 1

Recruiting Sergeant or Front Line Lieutenant

Being a twin has its delights and its drawbacks. As kids, Don and I were identical and inseparable. Even our mother called us "Dicky-Don."

Up through high school we did everything together. In any difficulty we were right there to help one another. Don helped me in math . . . I helped him in football. The time we sent the kids and faculty to the windows gasping for fresh air, I unlocked and opened the fan room door and Don threw the rotten egg into the whirling ventilator fans.

And as young marrieds, we used to enjoy spoofing each other's wives over the phone, for even now Don and I still speak alike.

The years have changed us. My hairline recedes while Don's waistline expands. Don has mellowed and grown benevolent while middle age has increased my physical problems. We have served God continents apart, and it seems incredible to us that some people still confuse us.

Don and I both accepted Christ as our personal Savior about the same time and both committed our lives to Him for foreign service while attending

DR. DON W. HILLIS
Missionary to India for fifteen years
Now Associate Director of
The Evangelical Alliance Mission

Biola. Graduation brought our first long separation as twins ... I was accepted by the China Inland Mission, and it was eleven years before I saw my twin again.

Don and I were raised in a Christian home in western Washington. Mother was a woman of prayer. Dad, a great ox of a timberman, knows the West Coast from the Mexican border to the Aleutians and loves the Bible from Genesis to Revelation.

We boys were taken to church from the time we were infants, but "familiarity breeds contempt." Even our going to a Christian school was a bit of a miracle. Don seemed to feel the ministry would be an honorable profession, so with a "Let's get on with the job" attitude he rode Greyhound from Seattle to Los Angeles and signed up. Several weeks later I followed Don but with no greater motivation than the multiple attractions of a big city over a little one.

While at Biola Don began to talk about India. "Dick," he said as we sprawled on our bunks for an evening bull session, "why do we have so many missionary speakers from China and South America and Africa, and yet it's been four months since we heard a speaker from India?"

"Maybe the India missions don't give their men furloughs," I suggested.

"No joking, Richard," he chided, wrinkling his forehead and running a hand through his wavy brown hair. "It bothers me. You know the old story of ten men carrying a log, nine men at one end and one at the other? Not much doubt at which end I ought to help."

"You think God wants you in India, Don?"

"Maybe. What about you?"

"I think God wants me in China. Don, if you go to India maybe we will get together. At least we will both be in the Orient."

As Don spent time seeking God's will for his life, he came across Jeremiah 1:5. The last phrase gripped him, ". . . I ordained thee a prophet unto the nations." The words lit up Don's path. God was leading him to lands beyond the seas. Then he stumbled on the

Word "India" (Esther 1:1) in his Bible reading. The whole context faded into insignificance and the one word stood before him in third dimension.

Is that guidance? you wonder. A rather presumptuous application to oneself of a tag-end of a Bible verse and a single word out of context. But remember, Don was praying and praying honestly. When you pray, you aren't in a position to quibble about the means by which God answers. God's guidance is ours, not by right but by grace. Don had the sense to recognize God's answer and the humility not to go on begging for more certainty.

Instead, he did the next thing. He began a careful study of mission boards. At that time there weren't many American missions serving in India. After almost a year of prayerful study, Don decided to apply to the Ceylon and India General Mission.

Don's mission board advised him to go to college. While at Wheaton, he filled a student pastorate to keep himself in fighting trim for front-line work abroad. But something happened to his missionary goals.

I had been in China four years when Mother wrote that Don had withdrawn his application to the Ceylon and India General Mission. Don was finding great acceptance in youth meetings and now felt that rather than go to the foreign field himself he should stay home and be used of God to stir others to go . . . a "Don Hillis recruiting agency" as it were.

Now wait a minute. Had not Don already asked God for guidance about where God wanted him to serve? Had not God given him a verse about being "ordained a prophet to the nations"? And here he is facing the same question all over again.

Yes, we human beings often have to refight the same old battles to recapture the same ground. The temptation we think we have licked is the one that knocks us for a loop. It is rather bewildering at times. And few missionaries last out even a first term without seriously questioning their "calling" and confronting all over again the challenge, "Is this really where God wants me?"

Personally, I could not condemn my brother's irresoluteness too harshly. As a first term missionary I was reeling from bitter defeats. I was fighting and losing the old battle of language. Succumbing to loneliness and discouragement, I would have given anything for a successful Stateside ministry.

But a few weeks later Don wrote, "Dick, your brother, as usual, has made a fool of himself. For a year now I have been thinking of myself as God's answer to the needs of American young people. With the solid help of well-meaning friends I have come to consider myself indispensable to the church here. And think of the young people I could influence to go to India if I would stay in the States!

"Yielding to pride within and pressure without, I withdrew my C.I.G.M. application. But how miserable I was. I went through weeks of restlessness. We talk a lot about the peace of God but, man, nothing teaches one what peace is, like going without it.

"I have now applied to The Evangelical Alliance Mission and am on my way to some place named Khandesh. It is kind of scary, Dick, but great to be back on the right track again."

For Don the right track led to India. Orientation, language, a hundred and one adjustments followed by a thousand and one battles. Then fifteen years of preaching to the lost and teaching and edifying the saved. Don does not claim to be a great missionary but his letters revealed that he had a great time being a missionary.

* * * * *

You want to be sure you are on the right track or you will never reach God's goal for you. How do you find that track?

In the fascinating biographies that follow, you will hear men ask that same question. Watch, and you will be surprised at the variety of ways God guided them. And how often the deciding straw was a little thing—a Scripture text on the wall, the chance word of a friend at church, a magazine article, a party place card. But each time God's guidance came with divine force, the assuring power of His Spirit.

For most of these men and women, the problem is not so much a problem of *knowing* as a problem of *willing*. Each of us faces a crisis of the will. Like stubborn padlocks, we stick at some point. It may be location . . . vocation . . . language . . . marriage . . . or a dozen other things.

Our specific block may seem as out of proportion to the consequences as the eating of some fruit to the loss of Paradise. The real issue for each of us is whether we will open our lives to God. Will we obey God or not?

To each one in this book the choices presented are different. One man is asked to postpone his marriage for five years. Another fears he may have to give up basketball. Paul had to decide between a Greek major and pre-med training. Norm is asked to audition for the Jack Benny show. Bill's choice seems almost absurdly insignificant—which seat will he take at the dinner table?

I have tried to tell their stories in the vocabulary the men themselves would use so that you can step inside and see the problems they faced from their own point of view. But you will want to interpret the stories in the terms that fit your experience— commitment and consecration.

CHAPTER 2

"Don't Interfere with My Plans"

Would God ask him to give up basketball? Bud tried to put the nagging question out of his mind as he dribbled the ball across the court. He hollered to some of his teen-age chums. They trotted over to shoot baskets with the school's star cager.

Their noisy comradeship only temporarily drowned the battle Bud Schaeffer was fighting. Was he willing to surrender completely to God?

By all normal standards, Bud ran his own life successfully enough. His high school buddies voted him junior class vice president, senior class president, president of the hundred-voice glee club, and "most likely to succeed." He spent his stint with the Navy playing basketball on their Great Lakes squad against Big Ten schools.

In college he led his class during his freshman and senior years as president and for four years was chosen for the All-Conference basketball team. Little All-American honors and a year of pro-ball followed. There was no question about Bud's ability on his own.

But God had early laid claim to Schaeffer's life.

BUD SCHAEFFER
Little All-American basketball player
Coach of Venture for Victory basketball team
Coach of Chinese Olympic Team in 1956
Missionary with Overseas Crusades, Inc.
in the Philippines
and Australia

Would Bud yield God everything, even his love for basketball and his yen for a machinist's career?

As a youngster, Bud Schaeffer was torn between the ways of his father and his mother. Bud's mother regularly took her children to a Gospel Tabernacle where Beryl, Bud's older sister, became his Sunday school teacher. Mr. Schaeffer lost five houses to the bank during the depression. Being a bartender, he had access to a quick cure for all his woes, and Bud saw him drunk more often than sober.

Bud ran around with a gang of junior high boys who vaunted their maturity, as boys do, by smoking and by committing acts of impudent vandalism. Following his dad's example, young Schaeffer used to stay up all night gambling. Then on Sundays he had to go to church with his mother and Beryl, where he would squirm through Sunday school and the morning service.

He was thirteen when the preaching of the Word hit home. As conviction deepened, he knew he must make his decision. But what would his friends think? When the invitation was given, with characteristic courage, Bud went straight to the altar to put his trust in Christ.

"As I walked out of that meeting," Bud recalls, "it seemed like the angels were singing right above my head. I had accepted Jesus Christ and He had accepted me."

Then tragedy struck. Bud's mother died. The sudden disaster brought his bartender father to his senses, and he was wonderfully converted and surrendered his life to God.

"Both my dad and I were looking for satisfaction at the wells of this world," Bud explains, "and we always went away thirsty until we drank of the Water of Life, Christ Himself."

Though Bud accepted Christ's salvation, he had some reservations about Christ's control. Bud wanted to play basketball and to be a machinist. Did dying to self mean giving up the ball court and the machine shop? Let Bud describe his conflict:

"I felt that God would have me go into the ministry, but I never told anyone. For two years I had a tremendous struggle in my heart. To me, going into the ministry was the most difficult thing I could imagine! I had over 1500 hours of high school machine shop work to my credit, and I didn't want the Lord to interfere with my plans.

"My prayers went something like this: 'Lord, I don't seem to be willing to do absolutely anything You want, but I pray that You'll make me willing. If necessary, Lord, even knock me down on the flat of my back and cause me to die if I'm not willing, but somehow, make me willing.'

"With boyish practicality, I was pretty sure God would never take such drastic measures. While I was in the Navy at the age of eighteen, after hearing a message that wasn't even about dedication, I slipped out of my seat and yielded my life for the ministry."

That act of surrender rang the curtain on Bud's machine shop work, but his basketball career was still in Act One. At Wheaton College, Bud's prowess on the court kept his fans constantly amazed. "Unbelievable Bud" they called him.

When Bud had the ball no one could keep him away from the basket. Confronted with an opponent, one of his favorite tricks was to break his dribbling pace and send a high bounce over the man's head. Round the startled player he swooped to catch the ball on the jump and toss it through the hoop in one swift motion. Sometimes he would slam it against the backboard, catch it going full speed and shoot while still in the air. But more than being a "ball hog," he was a sparkplug for teamwork.

The pro teams made bids for Bud's services when he graduated, and Schaeffer spent a high-speed year on a team called the Boston Whirlwinds (now Celtics) playing exhibition ball against the world-famous Harlem Globetrotters team in forty different states and Cuba.

In the one game that the Whirlwinds defeated the Globetrotters out of the fifty or so games they played against them, Bud got one-third of his team's points when they won, 51 to 47, in Havana, Cuba.

Afterwards the owner and coach of the Globetrotters, Abe Saperstein, asked Schaeffer to be a member of the United States All Stars which was to tour South America for nine weeks, playing against the Globetrotters. Bud reminded Abe that if he did he would not play on Sunday. Saperstein still insisted that he go.

Bud married talented, artistic Alice Brown one week later, and after a two-week honeymoon he flew to South America to begin the tour. While in Rio de Janeiro, Brazil, the teams played before fifty thousand people at one game, up to that time the largest paid attendance to witness a basketball game. While the team was in Buenos Aires, Argentina, President Juan Peron and his beautiful wife, Eva, went to the game at Luna Park Stadium.

Immediately afterwards the Perons gave a cocktail party for the teams. Due to his convictions about drinking, Bud remained outside the room passing out Gospel tracts to the policemen sent there to guard their leaders.

After half an hour, Eva Peron emerged and saw Bud standing outside in his shiny yellow-orange uniform. She extended her hand to him. Just that morning, Bud had read, "I will speak of thy testimonies also before kings, and will not be ashamed" (Psalm 119:46). Reaching into his jacket pocket he pulled out a tract in Spanish, "Five Things God Wants You to Know."

As Madame Peron received it, she said in Spanish, "Oh, do you want my autograph?"

Schaeffer said in Spanish, "No, this is for you."

"Oh, thank you!"

As she went out the door, Bud prayed that her woman's curiosity and the Holy Spirit would not let her rest until she read it carefully. Later Bud learned that just the day before she had spoken to hundreds of thousands of people in Buenos Aires and millions more on the radio, saying, "My husband Juan is god. Heaven would not be heaven without my husband. He is the very air we breathe." One year later she died of cancer.

Now it was time to give up basketball and prepare for the ministry. Bud enrolled at Fuller Seminary. His first year he was chosen president of his class.

In 1950 Bud toured Europe as song leader and

soloist on a Gospel team. In the summer of 1952, Coach Don Odle asked Bud to travel with the first Venture for Victory basketball team to the Orient. As well as for their playing ability, members are chosen for their Christian experience and musical and speaking abilities.

Schaeffer states: "I'm thankful that in 1950 I had the hottest night I ever had on a basketball court the last game of my Wheaton College career when we played Taylor University. I was able to hit eleven of twelve long shots from the middle of the court. No doubt this was one big reason (if not the main reason), other than my Christian testimony, that Coach Don Odle asked me to join the rest of the Taylor team that first year out to the Orient."

Still Bud had no intention of being a foreign missionary. He had yielded his life to the Lord for full-time ministry, and it was up to God to show him where that ministry should be. The Venture for Victory summers of 1952 and 1953 cinched the answer to Bud's old question. Did God want him to give up sports? No, God intended him to use his basketball ability as a wedge to open doors to the Gospel in the Far East.

Basketball had never been tried to the extent the first Venture for Victory team planned to use it for evangelism. No one on the team or those arranging the schedule knew whether or not it would work. Most of the games and meetings were planned for the island bastion of Formosa. Preachers or missionaries could not gain entrance into the schools and army camps for evangelistic purposes, but since basketball was the number one game, a team from the United States was very welcome. That first summer the team played eighty-seven games. It was not unusual for over two hundred soldiers, sailors, air force men, or students to remain after the game, bow their heads and ask Christ to forgive their sins.

Often the team played three games a day, even with some players sick because of the heat, food, water, or travel. But Bud says he will never forget the joy of lying down at night and realizing that that day hundreds of precious souls had opened their hearts to the Savior on the basketball courts. He and the team looked forward to every game. They were constantly amazed at the way basketball opened up doors for the Gospel.

Now located in the Philippines, the 180-pound six-foot athlete scores high with the Orientals. Bud and Alice sometimes team up together in singing and witnessing, Alice with her colored chalk and singing ministry. Schaeffer witnesses to God's saving power with all the drive and enthusiasm that made him a professional ball player. A wide grin slashes his angular face as he presents Christ to a pedicab driver, a college professor, or a teen-age sports fan.

"Basketball evangelism" is our name for the kind of work Bud does. In ten years of missionary service Bud played over six hundred games. Each one gives opportunities for preaching at half time and personal counseling later. Basketball clinics get Schaeffer into high schools as short-term coach.

For four months in 1956, Overseas Crusades loaned Schaeffer to the Chinese Nationalist Olympic Committee, which was preparing their teams for the Olympics in Melbourne, Australia. Coaching the Chinese basketball squad was exciting work.

"Lots of spring in those legs. Head up. Follow through! Good! Watch the wrist action next time," coaches Schaeffer, catching the ball as it swishes through the net and sending it back with a bounce to the keyhole where little Mr. Chu, Chinese All-Star, is perfecting his free-throw technique.

The next ball teeters on the rim, then drops beside the basket. "You're tired," laughs Bud, retrieving the ball.

"And hot," admits Chu, wiping his forehead. In the humid, tropical summer the cotton uniforms of both men stick to their damp skins.

Schaeffer reaches for a bottle opener and opens two bottles of "Aerated Water," the popular Formosan soft drink. The two men sit on the first rung of the empty bleachers and talk over the prospects of the coming game.

"Want to work on that one-hand jump shot?" asks Schaeffer, depositing the two empty bottles in the case. But Chu is glad to have the coach alone for a minute. Something has been puzzling him.

"Mr. Schaeffer, Sir, I don't understand what you are doing in the Orient. With your ability, you could be playing pro-ball or coaching in a Big Ten school in the States. You could make money—lots of it. Out here you coach us for nothing. It doesn't make sense to me."

Bud's eyes sparkle with anticipation. He knows Chu well enough by now to know just where to meet him. "You are a jet pilot, Mr. Chu. What kind of flying do you do?"

Mr. Chu tells of the twenty missions he has flown over Red China to drop leaflets encouraging the Chinese people to retain their hope for freedom.

"Were those missions dangerous?" asks Bud.

"Sure," admits Chu, "but national freedom is more important than personal safety."

"That's how I feel too," says Schaeffer. "Some things are more important than personal ambition." He proceeds to tell Chu the story of Jesus Christ's death for him.

Chu's dark eyes moisten as the cruelty of the crucifixion takes hold of his heart, and he responds with a barely-repressed shout to the glory of the resurrection. For the first time the old, old story means something to him. It is told him by a man he can trust, by a man whose whole life is a testimony to its practical power.

"Mr. Schaeffer, could you teach me how to be a Christian?" asks Chu after a pause.

Bud's smile seems to say, "Sure, man, that's just what I am here for."

Schaeffer's enthusiastic letters record spiritual victories as well as athletic, "A team member, small Mr. Chu, a jet pilot with twenty missions over Red China, accepted the Lord last week . . . others have expressed interest. Pray with me."

In another letter the Olympic coach writes, "The basketball team manager, Captain Tang, received Christ as his personal Savior yesterday. He came to church to hear me speak, and at the invitation came forward for Christ."

Most of the year Bud's missionary work in the Philippines is much the same as that of any other missionary. He is active in Bible classes, city-wide crusades, pastors' and laymen's conferences, and the ever-present opportunities in personal evangelism to point prepared men, women and youth to Christ.

But the summers are different. When June rolls around, Schaeffer moves his field of witness to the basketball court.

For ten summers Bud has played with the Venture for Victory team. This has taken him to fourteen countries of the Orient and has given him opportunity to witness to around five million people who, no doubt, would not have come under the hearing of the Gospel in any other way.

Bud never limits his witness to the half-time program. With heart and mind full of the Word, he maneuvers to instant witness whenever the Holy Spirit indicates the opportunity. With Schaeffer, witnessing involves not only words but life and attitude. Many times on the basketball court I have watched him answer a dirty play or a purposeful foul from his opponent with a smile. Bud never forgets that his vocation is witnessing for Christ. To him basketball is a delightful avocation that enables him to more completely accomplish his vocation.

When the Venture for Victory team does not go to the Orient, Bud gets together with a team of missionaries. The majority of the Crusaders team, as they call themselves, is made up of Venture for Victory alumni, men who went to play and stayed to preach.

"The men are aging," Bud admits, "and the Orientals are improving, but we can still play a pretty good brand of ball. To lose a game now and then doesn't hurt us. After all, it is not basketball we are bringing to the people of the cities and barrios. It is Christ."

Conditions under which the men play would be enough to make most men hang up their suits, but Schaeffer insists, "Circumstances become immaterial to us when we have the chance to talk to a spectator or a cager about Christ."

"Play in the rain?" Of course! At one game,

while the players slid from one end to another. the referee trotted up and down the court with a whistle in one hand and an umbrella in the other. At another game, Schaeffer helped dig small trenches to draw the water off the dirt court. Then, let her rain—the game must go on.

One court had the main road running across it, so every few minutes the whistle blew to give a logging truck temporary right of way. When the lights went out at one night game, the motorcycle police beamed their headlights at the team so they could continue their half-time preaching to the 3,000 spectators.

When I asked Bud why he was in the Orient, he answered my question by relating a personal experience:

"I was in a solemn communion service in the States where more than 1500 Christians were present. The elements were passed out and then the pastor asked, 'Is there anyone who has been omitted?' A missionary from India stood and said, 'Four hundred fifty million in India have been omitted.' A moment of hush was broken when a missionary from the Philippines stood, 'Thirty million of our people have been omitted.'

"This continued for some time as missionaries from different countries told of vast populations omitted from the Lord's salvation because no one had told them of Jesus Christ, the Way. Christ's death on Calvary was as much for them as for me and as long as God wants me to use a basketball to attract them and a BOOK to win them, I will do His will.

"And when God tells me to pass the ball on to somebody else and just use the Book, I will hang up my suit and be obedient."

CHAPTER 3

Christ's Enlisted Man

Charged by a wounded tiger . . . cornered by an infuriated wild boar . . . Donald McGavran has had his share of adventures.

He has traveled in six continents, canoed down the Congo River, shot tigers in India, climbed the Himalayas, trekked across remote parts of the Philippines, Ruanda, Kenya, and Brazil.

He has floated logs down river to build missionary hospitals. During fearful cholera and smallpox epidemics, McGavran, not an M.D., has treated hundreds. For years he superintended a leprosy hospital. He has made movies and written books translated into half a dozen languages and read in fifty countries.

He has founded a new kind of training program, the Institute of Church Growth, which is influencing a whole generation of new missionaries. His views on the strategy of missions are influencing many missionary societies today. He calls for research and experimentation and a more effective deployment of resources in the many populations which are receptive to the Gospel. How did this man become a missionary?

Donald McGavran looked to me more like a school

DR. DONALD A. McGAVRAN
Missionary to India under the United Christian Missionary
Society
Missionary strategist and founder of the Institute of
Church Growth
First Dean of Fuller Seminary Graduate School of Missions
and Church Growth

---

teacher than a missionary or a big game hunter. As he greeted me, I was impressed with the warmth of his handshake and the keenness of his glance. And though he spoke perfectly seriously, I noticed a smile lurking at the corners of his mouth, under the scrub of his salt-and-pepper moustache.

"Our stories start before we are born," reflected Dr. McGavran when I queried him about his missionary calling. A third-generation missionary, Donald inherited a wealth of missionary experience and know-how. His Grandfather Anderson went to India in 1854 with his young wife. In those days India was a white man's grave. No one knew the cure for plague, cholera, malaria, dysentery, and many other tropical diseases.

The Andersons, Baptist missionaries in the mission William Carey started, sailed around Africa's southernmost Cape of Good Hope on a tedious six months' trip to India. They were almost killed in the Indian mutiny of 1857.

Donald's grandfather had driving energy and a scholarly mind. He spoke both Bengali and Hindi fluently. When he developed tuberculosis he did not give up in despair. He simply moved to a drier part of India and went right on working. He was one of "Christ's enlisted men."

Donald's father, too, was an enlisted man. He knew he was in God's army, carrying out God's orders. He grew up on a farm in northeastern Ohio. He and his sister Mary sold their farm to get an education. They both became missionaries of the Christian Churches to India. Mary, a medical missionary, died in India in the line of duty.

In 1913, after twenty years in India, Donald's father was called to teach missionary candidates at the College of Missions in Indianapolis. It was a rewarding academic assignment in pleasant surroundings, but by 1922 he felt God directing him back to India for a last term of seven years.

Even a casual glimpse at father and grandfather, and one realizes the high sense of duty they both possessed. But a sense of duty does not automatically descend to son or grandson. How then did Donald McGavran come to dedicate himself to Christ?

Growing up in such a family, Donald simply took it for granted that reasonable human beings did what pleased God, not themselves. His parents did not preach at him. They simply lived that way. The children saw that the committed life paid rich dividends in achievement, joy, and excitement.

Even so, Donald did not just "naturally become a missionary." As he considered his future and looked at his family, he felt they were overly "enlisted." They were *too* different from other people—his neighbors, teachers, schoolmates, and men of influence in the community.

"My parents' loyalty to Jesus Christ," says McGavran, "for a time worked to keep me from fully enlisting in Christ's service."

When he was fourteen, Donald confessed Christ as his Savior and was baptized in the First Christian Church in Tulsa, Oklahoma, but, so to speak, kept his fingers crossed. He was going to be a Christian all right but not a minister or a missionary. Through high school, college, and two years of soldiering in World War I, Donald clung to this determination.

During this time, he attended church and Sunday school regularly. While at the Downey Avenue Christian Church, he helped establish a Christian Endeavor Society. Even in the army, from 1917 to 1919, he lived, talked and worshipped so that his buddies knew he was a Christian.

Donald was grateful for his Christian upbringing. The habit of doing some things just because they were right and not doing others just because they were wrong was one he never regretted having learned. At the same time he sometimes resented the fact that his father, as a missionary, had been so poor. The family was forever economizing, it seemed. To help the children get through college, the McGavrans walked or rode streetcars while other people bought automobiles.

Young McGavran would say to himself, "My father has done enough for the Lord. It is time for me to strike out for myself and earn some money."

Law particularly attracted Donald as a career. He was a good student, a sharp debater, with enough leadership potential to win class presidency his senior year at college. Yes, he could succeed in law and live on Easy Street.

In his own words, "I'll be a good conventional Christian, but making money is my first purpose. The church needs Christian businessmen too."

Then how did Donald McGavran get to the mission field?

About this time, the successful college senior began to question the truth of the Christian religion. The regularities of nature, the laws of chemistry, physics, and psychology seemed to eliminate the necessity of any other world explanations. Was a personal God possible? Could an educated man hold to the authority of the Bible?

McGavran decided that in the interests of truth he would have to give up his Christian faith.

But were his doubts really the result of his growing scientific knowledge? No, he confessed, when he faced the matter squarely. If honesty and truth were so important to him, he would have to admit that the source of his doubting was an inner debate —"If I don't give up Christianity altogether, I may have to give up money-making as a life goal."

The half-and-half life just did not hold water logically. Only by denying Christianity entirely could he reject the demands of Christ on his life.

So it was all or nothing. What the "all" would be he had seen in his parents and grandparents. "Nothing," the life of self-seeking, he had seen in some of his classmates and fellow GIs. A flat life, a life without transcendent dimensions, without— when he looked at it honestly—even the richness of the possibilities that faith opens on the terrestrial plane.

McGavran chose to surrender to Christ, and the great adventure began. With his heart set toward the mission field, he went to Yale Divinity School.

He graduated cum laude in 1922, married lovely Mary Elizabeth Howard, and in September, 1923, sailed for India under the United Christian Missionary Society. For several years their work was educational, managing the high school and grade schools their mission maintained in that area.

In 1937 they were assigned to "district work."

For the next seventeen years, they did everything that had to be done in the Takhatpur area—evangelism, schools, leprosy home, agricultural demonstration, and building. But their main concern was planting Christ's church in the villages of the densely populated plains of Mid-India. These were good years, filled with excitement and adventure, and much routine.

McGavran is reluctant to talk about the adventures of his missionary career. "There is always more routine than excitement," he insists. "For every hour of battle there are months in the barracks. For every scientific breakthrough there are years of patient research."

But when I pressed him to tell me about some of his exciting experiences, he obliged me with this story:

"No tiger hunt ever made such demands on me as trying to get a church started in the Indian village of Takhatpur. Because there was no former contact with Christianity, there was opposition. All kinds of false rumors circulated. After people became Christians, the whisper ran, their children were kidnaped and had their livers extracted and sent to America.

"Feudal lords, afraid that their laborers after becoming Christians would forget their lowly station in life, warned them, 'It won't be healthy for you to become Christians.'

"Yet, as our team of nationals and missionaries lived in a town or village for ten days and then worked and conversed, and preached, we saw people attracted to Christ and to His salvation. Clearly, many wanted to be Christians. For the first time in their lives they saw the possibility of victory over sin, freedom from evil spirits, and certainty of life after death. The very attractiveness of Christ drew them.

" 'If He gave His life for us,' the men said earnestly, 'we must gratefully worship Him. Tell us how to be Christians. We will follow Jesus even to death.'

"What a thrilling time! Public meetings, secret meetings, pacts between brothers and cousins to be baptized on the same day. How we prayed and yearned over every seeker! Some followed through.

Some failed to. Each decision carried eternal significance.

"This was more exciting than hunting tigers and intensely more meaningful. A church was in the process of being established. We were involved and absorbed in a struggle for the souls of men, and life seemed sharp, vivid, dramatic, keyed to the highest pitch. This is high adventure. There is nothing like it. I praise God for letting me share in scores of adventures like this."

Pastoring the congregations was also exciting at times. In one rural congregation, the feudal lord, in the protracted absence of Occutt, who had become a Christian, razed his house to prevent his ever returning. Since Occutt had clear title to the lot, redress by law was possible but prohibitively expensive.

Thirty Christians from neighboring villages gathered materials, carried them in, built a house on the lot, moved Occutt's family into it, lighted a fire, and set some food cooking. Tearing down an occupied house was, they held, something even a feudal lord would not dare to do. They marched into the village at daybreak, McGavran with them, carrying a couple of poles, and built the house in three hours.

The feudal lord, infuriated at the frustration of his plans, rounded up his goons to give battle. Since they were only five and the Christians were thirty, however, he thought better of it and sent a runner to call the police officer who lived five miles away and who was greatly indebted to the feudal lord because of past favors. The officer came galloping on his horse, charged McGavran with inciting riot, and arrested him.

The case dragged on for months. McGavran was warned never to walk anywhere alone and especially never to visit that village congregation or he would be beaten and killed by the strong men. Believing he had done no wrong, and confident in the Lord's protecting care, however, he continued to visit other congregations and the village of the new hut too, walking or cycling as the case might be, and usually alone. No hand was ever raised against him. Finally the case was settled out of court and dropped. Brother

Occutt remained in his house and the village congregation signed a promise never to construct a church on his desirable corner lot!

Later when the feudal lord fell seriously ill, McGavran took him to the mission hospital in the jeep. Upon his recovery he became a fast friend of the church. Though he never became a Christian, he attended the dedication of the church building a few years later.

"Missionary life was seldom dull," says McGavran.

When I asked Dr. McGavran if young people today could have the same leading in their lives that he experienced, he quickly answered:

"Yes, of course. God has a plan for every life. He drew up the plan for me and gave me strength and wisdom to follow it. All I did was accept His guidance. He will do the same for all who trust Him.

"To be quite honest, however, sometimes I did not accept God's plan fully. Mine would have been a better life if I had been more sensitive to His leading and done it more faithfully. But I did accept the Bible as the inspired Word of God and when God said, 'You shall have no other gods before me,' I said, 'Yes Sir.'

"As I accepted the Bible and determined to do what God wanted me to do, His will became clear. Certainly it takes faith to believe that becoming a Christian makes an eternal difference. One has to believe the Lord is literally 'the Pearl of great price,' the gain for which a man gladly sells all he has and can never lose.

"That is how I became a missionary, and I am still becoming one. Being a missionary is a continuous process. God has had a series of projects for me. One chapter closes and another opens. Some day this earthly chapter will close and a new one will open in heaven. That will be the most exciting adventure of all."

CHAPTER 4

Irresistible Logic

Collegians from New York to California are agitated into action by Dr. Arthur Glasser's searching questions and forthright mission challenge.

Even students who are complacent about their personal responsibility to participate in world evangelism admit that they are compelled to listen to his logical and orderly presentation. He speaks with conviction, they say; and conviction, like acid, leaves its mark.

I first met Dr. Glasser and his attractive wife Alice in Southwest China. It is a long bike ride from his birth place in Paterson, New Jersey, to the near border of Tibet. And it is a long mental jump from civil engineering, for which Glasser was trained, to missionary service. But when I stepped inside the Glasser home on that eventful day in 1946, I shook hands with a civil engineer turned missionary.

How is it that today Glasser is a seminary dean and not an engineer? In the study of engineering did he lose his way or was it all part of a divine pattern? What spiritual cables strung the suspension bridge from New Jersey to Yunnan . . . from engineering to missionary service? Such questions lift their heads and clamor for answers.

Arthur was born the year (1914) that Kaiser Wil-

DR. ARTHUR F. GLASSER
Missionary to China under the China Inland Mission
Home Director of Overseas Missionary Fellowship
Dean, School of World Mission, Fuller Seminary

helm led his nation into war. John E. Glasser, his father, was a very successful lawyer of Swiss-German extraction. His mother, Clara Weise, of strong but gentle nature, was German born. Although Glasser's father was from a Swiss Reformed Church background and his mother of the exclusive Plymouth Brethren, they were content to rear their son in what Arthur calls "a rather liberal Presbyterian church."

Young Glasser's teen years were academically successful and happy. At both the public schools of Paterson and the Augusta Military Academy in Fort Defiance, Virginia, his facile mind and verbal acuity won the respect of students and faculty alike. He was popular and his grades above average, but more than popularity and grades were necessary to satisfy this youth. He longed to build and create, to bridge chasms and span turbulent rivers.

During those teen years, he recalls, "I lived largely without the least concern about spiritual matters. Jesus Christ meant nothing to me."

Then in June, 1932, he was invited by his older brother John, recently converted at Princeton University, to attend a student conference at American Keswick in New Jersey. Though only mildly interested, he decided to go. At the conference he encountered Jesus Christ . . . but I will let Arthur tell his own story:

"My conversion experience at Keswick was quite overwhelming with the issue of the Lordship of Christ crucial to my understanding of what it meant to be among His followers. My manner of life was completely transformed because of the awareness that I was no longer my own; I had been 'bought with a price.' "

Before this life-changing experience, Arthur had set his heart on becoming a civil engineer. Now with a spiritually-charged battery he became deeply involved in Christian activities, both on and off the Cornell campus. In 1936, he graduated with a degree in civil engineering and went right to work for the contracting division of Dravo Corporation in Pittsburgh, Pennsylvania.

Arthur found the work creative and exciting. Yet he was disturbed with the growing suspicion that God wanted him to leave engineering and go into full-time ministry. If this conviction were of God, he must obey. To discover whether it was God speaking to him he must act . . . and act he did.

He resigned his position and applied to the Moody Bible Institute. Upon graduation in August, 1939, he went to Faith Theological Seminary and completed his work for a B.D. degree three years later. During these four and a half years of formal training, Glasser made it a point to become acquainted with missionaries and mission boards. Feeling the shove on his shoulder to serve God in a foreign land, he made a tentative offer of himself to the China Inland Mission.

Recalling his steps he candidly admits, "My first approach to the China Inland Mission was rebuffed for lack of clear evidence on my part that God had called me to this organization."

Still pondering the issue of foreign missions, Glasser became a U.S. Naval chaplain. And what did three years of naval service mean to the young engineer turned missionary candidate?

Arthur tells us, "While serving in the Southwest Pacific in the First Marine Division the Lord began to confirm that the earlier sense of drawing to the China Inland Mission was from Him. When again I knocked at this door it opened to me."

In summarizing the factors that led to his decision to reapply for foreign service, Arthur says, "God used many factors to lead me to this decision: the teaching of the Scriptures regarding God's worldwide purpose; many contacts with missions, their missionaries, activities, and literature; and the specific response of the Lord to my prayer to Him for guidance."

In Yunnan, Glasser's longing to be a bridge builder at last found satisfaction. With Chinese brush, rice paper and a Chinese-English dictionary, he labored to bridge the chasm of communication that divides East and West. Then with alert mind he constructed spans of truth across the gulfs of ignorance, fear and sin that severed his Chinese neighbors from God.

The engineer missionary was building a highway for his Lord. He was straightening crooked paths, filling in valleys, and making the rough places smooth so that "all flesh shall see the salvation of the Lord."

Up to this point in Glasser's story one is impressed with how easy it all seems. One discovers personal discipline and preparation and prolonged delays in reaching the field but no real problems . . . problems such as you and I face today. But his story is not finished, and before we jump to wrong conclusions we will do well to let Dr. Glasser continue:

"At every twist and turn in the way of discipleship and preparation for overseas service, there were obstacles to overcome and temptations to resist. How could it be otherwise? Nevertheless, there was always much grace and help from the Lord available to me. The path of duty and His call has always been made obvious to me by the illumination of the Spirit of God. Actually my *chief problem* at each point of decision has been over the issue of whether or not I truly desired to do His will.

"I cannot now honestly say that when crucial issues had to be faced and important decisions made my experience was one of darkness and uncertainty. No. God is faithful to me and always gave sufficient light for the next step."

As for pressures and possible detours, Glasser goes on to explain: "I could have bowed to parental pressure and not resigned my position in the engineering firm. I could have succumbed to the temptation to prolong my formal education through the G.I. Bill and thus pass by the possibility of overseas service. I could have allowed physical ailments arising from war service to hold me back. But the Lord triumphed instead because of His faithfulness."

And did Dr. Glasser have some crucial spiritual experience, some flash of light that led him into missionary service?

"Nothing out of the ordinary," he says, "but merely the irresistible logic of Scripture. Those whom God purchased on the Cross He calls. Those He calls He sends into His service—at home or overseas. If one 'covets earnestly the best gifts' he is soon caught up in the mighty ongoing purpose of God. In my case the constant renewal of Christ's first word to my heart, 'Forsake all and follow Me,' has enabled me to discover His will for my life and my day-by-day service and to do it."

With such commitment as this, are struggles eliminated? Glasser says not:

"My life has been one continuous struggle over the issue of obedience. Many a day has begun with my fickle, unstable heart clamoring for independence of God's control. But the command is to take the cross daily. This is possible by the power of the Holy Spirit. What results is the joy of discovering that the will of God can become daily something 'good, acceptable and perfect.' "

CHAPTER 5

Millionaire Missionary

Young William Borden had everything. More important, the young millionaire gave everything. In person he would carry the message of eternal life to dying men. By purse he would assist others to preach in foreign service.

William Borden's own missionary career lasted only four months. He arrived in Cairo, Egypt, in January, 1913, and died in April of the same year. He was just twenty-five years old.

When news of his death reached the States, the Richmond *Journal* said, "Even though he was cut off in his early prime before actually reaching his distant sphere of labor, it is doubtful whether any life of modern times has flung out into the world a more inspiring example."

Such a high tribute might be expected from his pastor or seminary professor, but it comes from the pen of a newspaper editor. An examination of his youth will pay dividends:

William Borden was born in Chicago, Illinois, on a cold November morning in 1888. Young Borden inherited some of his finest traits from his father, of Anglo-Saxon background. His ancestors were of Puritan stock. In exchange for religious freedom they gave up the comfortable life of the old world for the difficult life of the new world. His father, a tireless and suc-

WILLIAM BORDEN
Missionary to the Muslims under the
China Inland Mission

cessful businessman, provided affluently for his family.

Bill's mother had no less an influence on his life. In the book, *The Life That Counts*, Mrs. Howard Taylor says:

"There was something more than a distinguished ancestry that Mary Whiting Borden passed on to her son, William. When he was a lad of seven, Mrs. Borden entered upon a new experience spiritually which was to affect his life deeply. A devoted mother before, she now became an earnest, rejoicing Christian. To her, Christ was real and fellowship with Him satisfying in no ordinary degree. She found that she had gained not only peace with God but new zest in living, a new joy in home and loved ones.

"In the Moody Church, to which she transferred her membership, she found opportunities for service and the clear Bible teaching she coveted for her children. The result was very evident in the life of her younger son, who owed the strength and grasp of his spiritual conviction largely to that church home."

What did this move to the Moody Church mean to young Borden? Some years later he wrote, "I am very thankful for the teaching I received at the Moody Church and Institute before I was fifteen years of age, because it kept me firm in my beliefs in spite of opposition and criticism which I was not able to answer."

The actual date of William Borden's conversion is not clear, although two spiritual experiences are recorded. It is possible that through the first encounter he became acquainted with Jesus Christ as his Savior and through the second recognized the Lordship of Christ. In both cases God used that great Bible teacher, Dr. R. A. Torrey. The Moody Church pastor extended an invitation at the close of each service. In response to such an invitation, Bill, "a little fellow in a blue sailor suit," took his first step in open confession of Christ.

Several years later, as a boy of fourteen, William enrolled in the Hill School. Here he came under the strong influence of Dr. Meigs, a strict but kindly disciplinarian. He made his boys understand that the strength of noblest manhood was built on purity, not that Dr. Meigs trusted in moral training alone to develop the all-around manhood he had in view. A deeply religious man, he led the boys to seek after no artificial piety but a straightforward discipleship to Jesus Christ as Lord and Master.

Through his home training Borden arrived at the school well grounded in many of these principles. He was just sixteen when he graduated. For some reason unknown to us, his parents felt it would be profitable for William to travel a year rather than go directly into college. Therefore, with Mr. Walter Erdman as his escort, he began a trip around the world.

On this trip William again heard Dr. R. A. Torrey, this time in London, England. As he listened to Torrey's message, William realized that to accept Christ as Savior meant to accept Him as Lord. His conviction led to action and he started doing personal work.

That Sunday, July 2, 1905, in his diary he wrote, "Fine address. I was greatly helped and surrendered all to Jesus at the invitation."

The spiritual hunger William saw during his world trip shook him up. Upon his return to America he plunged into the absorbing academic life at Yale University.

Borden faced the same temptations as any other student but found the Word of God adequate in every case. He sensed the companionship of the Lord Jesus Christ and longed to share the reality of Christ with his fellow students. In order to witness, he started a Bible study among those who would not avail themselves of the influence of chapel or church.

Though intensely active in Christian work, not for a moment did he neglect his classroom assignments. In his junior year William's name appeared on the list of those who made Phi Beta Kappa.

Borden's college activities were summarized in the "Yale Alumni Weekly" as follows:

"He was President of Phi Beta Kappa. In athletics he was active in football, baseball, crew and wrestling, rowing on the winning team (1909), and playing on the winning Phi Beta Kappa baseball team. He served on the class Book Committee and on the Senior

Council. Elected a class deacon he devoted himself largely to religious work. He was unwilling to join any fraternity or secret society because he feared it might set him apart from the body of the class "

In 1909 Borden entered Princeton Seminary. In addition to a full academic program, Mrs. Taylor gives us a glimpse of his responsibilities outside Princeton:

"In the fall of 1909 he had been made a Trustee of the Moody Bible Institute in Chicago. In the spring of 1910 he was appointed a delegate to the Edinburgh Missionary Conference by the China Inland Mission, and in the fall was made one of the Directors of the National Bible Institute of New York City. He also became a member of the North American Council of the China Inland Mission and of the American Committee of the Nile Mission Press."

One cannot question that his home training, the careful teaching he received in church, and the world trip played a great part in turning Borden's steps toward missionary service. In reading his biography it is not difficult to put your finger on specific experiences that both kept Borden's feet upon the path and hurried him on the way.

While he was at school, the Student Volunteer Band started a work they called the Yale Hope Mission. William threw himself into the work of the mission.

Later Professor Henry Wright said, "It is my firm conviction that the Yale Hope Mission has done more to convince all classes of men at Yale of the power and practicability of Christianity to regenerate individuals and communities than any other force in the university."

A friend recalls, "Bill was the great example of one who seemed to realize always that he must be 'about his Father's business' and not wasting time in the pursuit of amusement."

During his freshman year at Yale he attended the Missionary Convention of the Student Volunteer Movement in Nashville. One speaker stood out above all others for Borden. He was a man with a map, charged with facts and enthusiasm, grim with earnestness, filled with a passion of love for Christ and the perishing. Samuel Zwemer made that great map live, voicing the silent appeal of the Mohammedan world.

William Borden seemed stunned with the new knowledge that there were more Muslims in China than in Persia, the whole of Egypt, and Arabia, the home and cradle of Islam. Born in his heart was an urgency and concern to enter China and reach its Muslims.

The year his father died he was a sophomore at Yale. That same year Borden offered himself for service to the China Inland Mission. Dr. Frost, the American Director, advised postponement, feeling Borden was too young (age nineteen). After graduation from Yale, once more Borden offered himself to the China Inland Mission. Again he was urged to defer the decision and to further his studies at Princeton. Toward the end of his time there he again offered himself to the C.I.M. This time his application was accepted.

Is there a reader who, once turned down by a mission board, has ceased all effort to get to the field? Like Borden, why not get up and start again? Not until Borden's third application was he finally accepted.

Examining his biography, one is struck by the fact that from the time of his conversion Borden's constant prayer was for God's will to be done in his life. His acceptance into missionary service with the China Inland Mission was just one step closer to that which he believed to be God's plan. Therefore, with controlled excitement, on December 17, 1912, he boarded the "Mauretamia" and sailed toward Cairo, not as a world traveler but as a missionary.

Less than four months after his arrival in Egypt, the news of his death was cabled to America. At that time the Princeton Seminary Bulletin wrote:

"No young man of his age has ever given more to the service of God and humanity, for Borden not only gave his wealth, but himself, in a way so joyous and natural that it was manifestly a privilege rather than a sacrifice."

CHAPTER 6

Counter-Espionage

David sat quietly in the beautiful Monkton Combe School chapel with about two hundred other boys. But he wasn't listening to the preacher. He was dreaming of China . . . that great and needy land!

David opened his Bible and studied the China map he had tucked inside. The population of China was represented by black squares with a tiny spot of white indicating the proportion of Christians.

One of David's favorite teachers had just left the boarding school to sail for China under the China Inland Mission. "O Lord," David prayed silently, "bless him. Give him a safe voyage and protect him from persecution."

David opened his gray eyes and studied the back of the boy ahead. He wondered if the Chinese still called white men "foreign devils." The book, *A Thousand Miles of Miracle in China,* describing the dramatic escape of C.I.M. workers from the terrors of the Boxer Rebellion, had captured the schoolboy's imagination. His mind wandered off into a recollection of the refugees' adventures until the bell recalled him to the mundane affairs of the school day.

He sighed and closed his book. "Wish I didn't have all this education to go through first," he thought. "If only I could be out in China right now."

David Adeney came by his missionary dream

DAVID H. ADENEY
Missionary to China under the China Inland Mission
Associate General Secretary for the Far East of the
International Fellowship of Evangelical Students

naturally enough. His father was a missionary to the Jews of Rumania, his aunt a missionary in Egypt. David had learned to trust the Savior at an early age and committed his life to God's direction during a summer camp by the seaside. There was nothing dramatic about his conversion nor about his early sense of missionary vocation.

But it takes more than youthful yearnings to make a missionary. Those years of preparation that David would rather have skipped had to be plodded through. The dreamlight had to be kept fueled with information, practical work, and prayer. For all too many children the "I'd-like-to-be-a-missionary" stage is one they outgrow along with the yen for cowboy suits and fire trucks.

David Adeney's is a story of faithfulness to an early vision, a story of training.

What did he need to learn between those dreamhours in school and his arrival on the Bund in Shanghai?

Thinking over David Adeney's formative years, I am reminded of Paul's instructions to another young preacher, Timothy. Paul's second short letter to his protege is full of pithy counsel (RSV, abbreviated):

"Do not be ashamed of testifying to our Lord.

"Do the work of an evangelist.

"Follow the pattern of sound words which you have heard.

"Guard the truth entrusted to you.

"Do your best to present yourself to God as one approved, a workman who has no need to be ashamed."

How did Adeney learn these lessons?

"For the Lord does not want you to be afraid of people, but to be wise and strong, and to love them and enjoy being with them. If you will stir up this inner power, you will never be afraid to tell others about our Lord..." (II Timothy 1:7, 8, *Living Letters*).

A missionary must not be timid. In inland China, Adeney would be something of a public spectacle, a milk-faced Westerner in a sea of tea-skinned Orientals. His large European nose would be a source of endless hilarity to the little bare-bottomed children who play in the village streets. He must learn to respond to the not-always-kind laughter with love, self-control, and the Holy Spirit's power.

Adolescents are notoriously self-conscious and, at eighteen, Adeney found it painfully embarrassing to create public notice. So the Missionary Training Colony stuck him up on a soap box at Tower Hill, happy hunting ground of London's professional hecklers, and told him to give his testimony.

This was not designed to be a private pillory for the sensitive lad. It was just part of the regular program of the Missionary Training Colony. After graduation from high school, Adeney joined the colony for an eight-month course which stressed intensive Bible study and practical evangelism. The men spent exhausting hours trying to reach the rough children of the London slums. In the evenings they took turns preaching in the open air at Tower Hill.

To make matters worse for self-conscious David, some of the men from the colony would cheer him on by shouting "Hallelujah" at the top of their voices. Everyone would look up to see what was happening as the "Hallelujahs" ricocheted across the street. Adeney, feeling hot and cold all over, would wish he were small enough to crawl under his soap box.

Of course, the men were only trying to be helpful. By and large the colony went out of its way to look after its youngest member. The discipline of the training program included a six o'clock cold bath, a run around the block, and an hour of private devotions before breakfast. The men took turns doing the cooking.

David's week as chef brought him another mortifying experience. He reduced the meatballs to cinders one night, but when he abashlessly sent the burnt offerings to the table, the men kindly choked them down.

Climax of the training program was a month of summer trekking. Pulling their own carts full of camping equipment, the men went out into the country to preach in the villages. Each night they spoke at a crossroads or in a market square, and on weekends they took meetings in churches and mission halls.

Finally the men were all paired off, given two shillings and a sixpence each, and sent out into unknown villages for a week. David's companion was an older man, one in whom the boy had real confidence. But Adeney could not help feeling apprehensive about the week ahead when he saw that a chunk of their pooled resources—less than a dollar—went for bananas and a loaf of bread for their first meal.

Before they entered the village, a farming community nestled rustically in a hollow among hedged hillsides, the two stopped for prayer. They prayed, not just for food but for opportunities to present the Gospel. That evening they discovered a little group of Christians meeting for prayer. The believers welcomed the two evangelists and invited them to lead meetings in the village for the week. So every evening, after the cows had been milked and the livestock fed, the farm folk clustered into the local chapel to hear the Gospel message.

Daytimes David and his companion would call at the cottages, chat with the farmers in their fields, or gather the village children for an hour of choruses and Bible stories. Meals were provided for the two visitors by the villagers, some too poor to offer their guests more than soup or potatoes.

Young Adeney admired his older companion's knack of dealing with the everyday problems of the country people. Whereas David had an idea and a Bible verse for every situation, the other man knew how to apply the Scripture with gentle sympathy and a wealth of loving good sense.

Realizing he might one day be assigned to rural missions in China, David made a serious effort to communicate with the country people. Adeney's looks betrayed his upbringing. His slight figure, his fine hands, his intellectual features belonged to the world of libraries and liturgy. But he could not be content to be just a "preacher boy" to the farmers and smiths of the little English village. He longed to share with them the class-obliterating love of Jesus.

Eight years later, David Adeney was in Honan, a wheat-growing province of central China. There his assignment lay among village churches. He biked as far as a hundred miles a day, visiting the pastors and country believers. Time and again the lessons learned in the Missionary Training Colony came to his rescue ... when embarrassment over his poor Chinese would have prevented him from testifying ... when he felt lost and out of place in the rural culture ... when he was tempted to worry about physical provisions.

The second stage of Adeney's preparation for China was his university education at Cambridge. Here Adeney's understanding of Christian life and doctrine was clarified. Here he made preliminary choices on questions of church affiliation, theology, and religious experience.

"Hold tightly to all the many kinds of truth I taught you, especially the faith and love Christ Jesus offers you," is Paul's advice to the young believer. "Guard well that splendid ability which God has given you as a gift through the Holy Spirit Who lives within you" (II Timothy 1:13, 14, *Living Letters*).

Just before entering the university David Adeney faced the first of the choices which "the many kinds of truth" seemed to indicate. He changed church affiliation.

Theological conviction triggered the move, which was a painful break with family tradition. But David's sense of missionary vocation was the deciding factor. A missionary needs a strong prayer fellowship behind him. In the staid piety of his home church David found no keen missionary vigor to support his own. He turned instead to a neighbor church which sent its young people out on weekends to witness on the streets.

At the university, other choices presented themselves. Adeney threw himself into the activities of the Cambridge Inter-Collegiate Christian Union. Several current religious trends were raising questions among the members of the Christian Union, local version of Inter-Varsity Fellowship.

Moral Rearmament, then known as the Oxford Group Movement, was in its formative years. Should the C.I.C.C.U. join forces with these ambassadors of morality? The young people were divided on the issue.

Some pointed to the effectiveness with which the Oxford Group was stirring up nominal Christians to lives of public confession, active witness, positive virtue, and regular prayer. Through house parties and parlor talks, the Moral Rearmament people shared their life-changing experiences, leading hundreds in the university community to a conversion of some kind.

All very well, so long as folks were being converted to Christ, not just to the Oxford Group. But, unfortunately, the theology of the movement was vague, oversimplified, and overgeneralized. M.R.A. had a lot to say about Christian experience—guidance, holiness, conversion, confession of sins, and testimony—but little to say about Jesus Christ. The Cambridge Christian Union decided not to give the new movement its wholehearted support.

For Adeney it was a matter of guarding the truth entrusted to believers by the Holy Spirit. Without a firm basis in the redemptive death and resurrection of God Incarnate, what good was any amount of religious experience?

But what precisely did Paul mean by referring to "the Holy Spirit Who dwells within us"?

Says Adeney: "Many people, during my university years, were seeking a deeper spiritual life. We often used to discuss various experiences and theories connected with the filling of the Holy Spirit. We realized how much we needed the Pentecostal ministry of God's Spirit. But how to make contact with this overflowing power?

"With the president of the Christian Union I had a wonderful time of prayer. We asked God not for the exact experiences of anyone else but for the gift of His indwelling Spirit in the measure that would best fill our own lives."

How was Adeney's prayer answered? Young people in four continents testify to the reality of the Holy Spirit in the ministry of David Adeney.

During his final year at Cambridge, Adeney studied theology. The prescribed textbooks reflected the liberalism of the early twentieth century. By this time, on campus David had a reputation as an evangelical. The Dean of his college would occasionally invite him up to his room to defend the evangelical position in a theological bull session.

Sometimes these impromptu discussions caught Adeney off guard. His readings left him floundering in questions and confusing doubts—too unsteady to stand up for the faith.

Says Adeney, "It was the fellowship of Christian men and the reading of works by conservatives who had grappled with the same problems which put me back on my feet."

Certainly defensive "guarding the truth" involves aggressively "following the pattern of sound words." Adeney advises students to acquaint themselves with the best in evangelical scholarship. There are reasons for our faith, and we have a responsibility to be able to answer those who demand a testimony from us.

College is a time for straightening out one's ideas. Adeney's thinking about the church, about theology, about religious experience needed the sifting of those four years. But he did not neglect to keep in shape practically as well as intellectually. The Cambridge Christian Union offered a flood of activities: a daily prayer meeting, a weekly Bible study, opportunities to witness in the market place, practical work in the Sunday schools and young people's fellowships of local churches, missionary breakfasts featuring speakers from overseas, and weekly prayer meetings for mission candidates.

Adeney immersed himself in the Christian Union program, was enriched by its fellowship, and served as one of its administrators. Summers he spent at the beaches in the seashore evangelism work of the Children's Special Service Mission.

During his last two years in England, David served as missionary secretary of the British I.V.F. About this time the Inter-Varsity Missionary Fellowship was formed. The slogan first attached to this Fellowship was closely connected to an experience that Adeney had on a visit to the Holy Land:

One Sunday morning, he was sitting by the side of the road that leads over the Mount of Olives.

From the rocky hillside he could look across the valley of the Kedron to the "Golden Gate" of Jerusalem, which leads directly into the former temple area.

As David looked at this gate, again and again there came into his mind the words of the Psalmist, "Lift up your heads, O ye gates; and be ye lift up, ye everlasting doors; and the King of glory shall come in" (Psalm 24:7).

That morning he had been reading about King David's flight from Jerusalem. King David had passed along the same road over the Mount of Olives, rejected and deserted by most of his followers. Not long after, however, following the victory over Absalom, he returned and the cry went up, "Why speak ye not a word of bringing the king back?" (II Samuel 19:10). It seemed to him that these words could indeed be applied to the missionary task of world evangelization.

At twenty-two, David Adeney was ready to apply to the China Inland Mission, by now with a more focused vision—student work in China. His aspiration bore fruit after World War II when he joined the China Inter-Varsity Fellowship. For four and a half years, the last fifteen months under Communist rule, he worked to establish Christian fellowship groups in many universities in China.

During those difficult months under the Communist government, Adeney spent much time encouraging the Christian students who were forced to attend indoctrination classes. During those days some students were converted and there was great rejoicing when a new brother or sister was introduced to the fellowship or when one who had denied the Lord was brought back to the Savior.

Exciting? What counter-espionage story could compare with the adventure of planting cells of Christian life in the hotbeds of Communist indoctrination?

Booted from China at last, Adeney joined the American I.V.C.F. staff as missionary secretary. In this new capacity he carried a major part of the responsibility for the great 1954 Urbana Conference. Later David was commissioned as Associate General

Secretary for the Far East of the International Fellowship of Evangelical Students.

Adeney's love of the Orient, his practical energy, his instinctive understanding of the university clan, his willingness to grapple with academic and intellectual problems won him quick rapport with collegians from Korea to India.

Yes, plenty of practical evangelistic experience in England and a sound university education had well prepared David Adeney for missionary service. But the China Inland Mission required a final year of training at mission headquarters in London.

Soon after his arrival at the training home, Adeney was called up before the Candidates' Committee.

"To my dismay," he recalls, "a report had been received from the doctor stating that I was not really strong enough for overseas service. I'll never forget the council meeting when the final decision was to be made. Would I be accepted for work in China?

"From childhood I have been a member of the Scripture Union. That morning in the Scripture Union passage for the day appeared the verse, '. . . and as thy days, so shall thy strength be' (Deuteronomy 33:25).

"After breakfast I was scheduled to have an interview with a C.I.M. council member who was a doctor. The usual room for such interviews being occupied, we looked for a vacant office. Entering an available room we saw on the wall the text, 'As thy days, so shall thy strength be.' "

Thus the Lord assured Adeney that in spite of the adverse medical report he was still to go to China. Sure enough, the mission council granted him permission to continue preparations for the Orient.

Continued preparations included study of Chinese customs and courtesies, the long history of the "Middle Land," church and mission backgrounds, and, above all, the Chinese language. Studies were interesting, but Adeney found the discipline of the mission training home rather irksome.

After the freedom of the Cambridge campus, things like hours and room inspection and pigeonholes for dinner napkins seemed ridiculous. David possessed a wee tendency to have everything in a muddle and an optimistic faith that it would all work out somehow anyway.

But at the C.I.M., slovenliness of life or thought was not tolerated. David was forced to prepare thoroughly for every speaking engagement. No careless reliance on his past experience would do. Before each meeting he had to turn in a work sheet that read like a lesson plan: "Type of Audience Expected, Motive of the Message, Detailed Outline, Clear Introductory and Concluding Paragraphs."

The astonishing discovery which Adeney made in the process was that he needed this kind of methodical discipline. Without it, his messages were a patchwork of loosely woven insights and platitudes. Conscientious planning gave new clarity to his preaching.

Centuries ago, Paul gave similar advice to Timothy: "Work hard so God can say to you, 'Well done.' Be a good workman, one who does not need to be ashamed when God examines your work. Know what the Bible says and means" (II Timothy 2:15, *Living Letters*).

The discipline of the year at C.I.M. headquarters in London was the capstone of Adeney's mission preparation. The years the schoolboy had wanted to skip were indispensable in the making of the missionary.

Missionary Training Colony had taught Adeney to testify fearlessly, to be unashamed of the Gospel. Cambridge had strengthened his understanding of the Word of truth. C.I.M. headquarters forced him to work carefully, doing his best for God's approval.

Of course, the lessons so obvious in retrospect were not at all evident to the daydreaming schoolboy. Most of them were not even clear as young Adeney was being taught. Only looking back can we see that God's lesson plans were as well thought through as the ones C.I.M. required of its missionary candidates.

That is why I dare be optimistic about your future. God's purposes for you may seem vague now, but who knows what fulfillment of your truest dreams may blossom from them?

Hang on . . . you are already on the way! Or to

put it in Paul's more formal words to Timothy:

"But you must keep on believing the things you have been taught. You know they are true, for you know that you can trust those of us who have taught you. You know how, when you were a small child, you were taught the holy Scriptures; and it is these that make you wise to accept God's salvation by trusting in Christ Jesus. The whole Bible was given to us by inspiration from God and is useful to teach us what is true and to make us realize what is wrong in our lives; it straightens us out and helps us do what is right. It is God's way of making us prepared at every point, fully equipped to do good to everyone" (II Timothy 3:14-17, *Living Letters*).

CHAPTER 7

The Rejoicing Crisis

"You a missionary?" Mr. Ridderhof laughed benignly at his youngest daughter. "Joy, darling, be reasonable!"

Mr. Ridderhof turned to the visiting Quaker missionary and explained, "Our Joy is much too loving and impractical to be a missionary. But you must meet our daughter Amy. What a fine missionary she'll make!"

Joy Ridderhof encountered the same reaction when she mentioned her ambition to her school friends.

"You in Africa?" they would chortle. "Oh, Joy, you're afraid of a frog. You'd never be able to live in Africa, with witch doctors and lions and pythons."

They were right, Joy admitted sadly. Her older sister Amy had all the qualifications for missionary service. But Joy could not do much of anything. Still, she clung wistfully to the dream of serving God in Africa.

Joy's dream was born as she listened to a missionary message when she was just five years old. A woman spoke about the needs of Honduras, and little Joy wished that some day she might go and tell foreign people about Jesus.

The stream of missionaries visiting in the Ridderhof home in Los Angeles kept Joy's dream alive

MISS JOY RIDDERHOF
Missionary to Honduras
Founder and Director of Gospel Recordings

and interested her particularly in Ethiopia and the Sudan.

Joy attended Bible school, spent two years in practical church work in Miami, and completed a degree in professional education at U.C.L.A. In the spring of 1930, Miss Ridderhof was ready to go to the mission field.

In the spring of 1930, very few Americans were going anywhere, except bankrupt. But Joy's God was not bankrupt. He sent her first to the very parish in Honduras whose needs had first aroused her compassion.

There the girl who was "too impractical" to be a missionary survived two revolutions and constant persecution with the triumphant testimony that "fierce battles lead to glorious victories."

Too sick to return to Honduras after her first term, Joy seized pick and shovel, hammer and nails, and turned a dirt-floored Los Angeles stable into a snug recording studio.

The girl who "couldn't do anything" mastered the technicalities of the finest recording equipment. She traveled from Alaskan igloos to stone-age New Guinea, recording the Gospel message in the languages of illiterate tribes.

The child who was afraid of frogs grew up to spend a year in the Philippine jungles. In the shanties of brown-skinned natives, she endured gekko lizards and monsoon rains.

The girl who was "too impractical" to be a missionary now directs a recording studio, pressing and processing plants, and a phonograph factory in Los Angeles. She supervises a hundred full-time workers, oversees branch offices in six countries, and trains and directs field workers.

"It is good," Joy admits, "I did not know in the beginning how vast the task was to be, but I did know that God had pledged His Word. Of Abraham He said, 'But Abraham never doubted. He believed God, for his faith and trust were strong, and he praised God for this blessing before it even happened. He was completely sure that God was well able to do anything He promised' (Romans 4:20, 21, *Living Letters*). Could I not accept this inheritance too?"

Through five million whirling discs in over three thousand languages and dialects, Joy Ridderhof's faith speaks to the world. Testimonies to new life through the recorded message pour onto her Los Angeles desk daily from the four corners of the earth.

What turned the wistful Ridderhof girl into a woman of victorious faith? In three stages Joy recounts the experiences that led to the founding of Gospel Recordings: the healing of her disposition, the follow-through of obedience, the secret of rejoicing.

When Joy was a child her friends and family good-naturedly disparaged her missionary ideals. But that did not bother school-girl Joy too much. She was not particularly concerned about her lack of ability or adaptability. One thing troubled her— her disposition.

Joy set high standards. Missionaries must be victorious Christians in everyday life, especially in their homes. Joy knew she did not qualify.

"I wanted to be good," she says, "but I was willful. I was often cranky and cross. I was self-ish, very critical, easily aggravated. I fussed at my mother and blamed her for things that weren't her fault. The manners of my brothers and sisters annoyed and embarrassed me. I quarreled with Amy, my closest sister."

To the Friends meeting that the Ridderhofs attended in Los Angeles there came old-fashioned fiery evangelists who preached the verities of sin, of righteousness, and of judgment. "One who is not holy will not see the Lord" (Hebrews 12:14, *Living Letters*), they thundered.

The text dug deeply into Joy's consciousness and convicted her of sin in the give and take of daily living. Impatience, short temper, irritation—were these normal traits for a child of God?

"You don't act like a Christian," said Joy indignantly one day, applying her high standards to her older sister.

"Neither do you," retorted Amy.

"No, but I expect to when I'm your age."

Yet Joy was no better as she grew older. She disappointed herself daily. Was she torturing her conscience unnecessarily? Going outside the Quaker fellowship, Joy found preachers who told her she could never expect anything more in this life than daily defeats.

Outside of her home, Joy seemed a model Christian. She invited her schoolmates to church youth classes and attended the meetings faithfully herself. She never let down the strict standards of her home and church, never once went to a movie theater. She was active in all sorts of Christian work—Bible clubs in the schools, prayer groups, Christian Endeavor, street meetings and city missions.

As soon as she enrolled at U.C.L.A., she hunted up other Christians and found a prayer group that met every morning. Joy made it her primary obligation in life to attend those 7:45 a.m. prayer meetings each day. The need to witness for Christ rested heavily upon her, and she forced herself to speak to other students about her Savior.

Christianity for Joy Ridderhof, college freshman, age twenty, was a list of arbitrary negatives and a parallel list of arduous obligations. And ever with her was the nagging consciousness of her failures at home.

Surrender? Of course the solution was to surrender her life completely to God. Joy tried it . . . no result. She went on praying, fretting, hungering.

During finals week, Joy was drawn away from her anxieties about her grades by a conference at the Friends church. Dr. R. C. McQuilkin was scheduled to speak on "The Victorious Life," basing his messages upon the book of Romans.

If the subject brought Miss Ridderhof to the first meeting, the speaker kept her coming. The assurance in his voice, the radiance on his face, the freedom and joy of his spirit gave a ring of reality to his words.

"What a surprise!" says Joy, describing the impact of those sermons. "Instead of harping on the sins of anger or bad temper, he bore down hard on the worst of my defeats—worry. 'Worry is a sin,' he would say.

"I was undone. With all my spiritual inadequacy I had thought that at least my concern for my own condition was commendable. But now I saw it for what it was—worry—a slap in the face of a loving, all-powerful God. No wonder my attempts at surrender hadn't worked. I'd never surrendered my right to fuss over my own spiritual life."

Sitting in the church, hearing the words "surrender" and "trust," Joy at last let go of her own efforts to live like a Christian. "It seemed as though I would fall over a steep precipice and be lost if I did, but the word 'trust' rescued me. I trusted that God's arms received me, that His Spirit had taken control."

For Joy Ridderhof, surrender was an act of the will, not an emotional experience. In the following months, as she watched God turn her into the kind of person she felt a missionary should be, her heart filled with gladness.

Miss Ridderhof likes to say that life began for her then. Immediately ahead of her lay seven years of training and patience and then a crisis of decision about her missionary call.

Several things in those years could have held Joy back from missionary service. A man she loved proposed to her. She turned him down because of her missionary commitment. Still, the desire to have a home and family pulled strongly. Later the friendship was renewed. Because Joy had no immediate plans for going to the field, she decided to say "Yes" to him but was prevented in the simplest possible way. He never popped the question.

For two years Joy did church work in Miami. In a fast-growing community, she saw much fruit among needy people. Lives were transformed. Prayers were answered. Young people were steered into Christian service. Should Joy remain in Florida and continue to serve God there? Perhaps some of the young people she influenced would become missionaries in her place.

But family needs in Los Angeles recalled Joy to the West Coast. There she turned her face once more towards Africa as she set to work to complete her studies at U.C.L.A. for a teacher's credential.

About to graduate, Joy looked around for missionary openings. There were none. The depression had closed the doors. Missions were considering retrenchment. What should she do? She had already bypassed marriage and a successful ministry in Miami.

Joy possessed a brilliant mind. Her high grades and recommendations brought her an invitation to teach in the Los Angeles school system. She was delighted. She could earn a comfortable salary in spite of the depression. She could save money for her missionary outfit. And she could help pay her own way to Africa.

When a college Bible class teacher asked Joy what she planned to do after graduation, Joy told her, "I'm going to teach for a year or two and then apply to the Sudan Interior Mission or Africa Inland Mission."

The teacher looked at Joy in surprise and said, "But you know the time is short."

Joy went home and faced the matter. She prayed, "Lord, if You want me to go abroad now, show me an open door before the date of entering into my contract with the city schools. If You will give me an opening, I'll go to the mission field." Of course, Joy meant she would go to Africa.

Several days later a member of her church asked Miss Ridderhof if she would be interested in working in Honduras under the Quaker Mission Board. A needy post was empty there.

"I was shocked," recalls Joy. "I almost felt like Jephthah with my rash vow. I was caught."

Joy Ridderhof felt no pull toward Latin America. As a little girl she had been afraid of Mexicans and would cross the street to avoid them in Los Angeles. She did not know any of the missionaries in the Quaker work in Honduras. Besides, she planned to apply to one of the interdenominational faith missions. Though they attended a Friends church, the Ridderhofs had never identified with the denomination.

Joy's heart was heavy. A strange country, strangers to work with, a denomination to serve, and of all fields, Latin America! But in the face of her promise to God, how could she refuse?

"I waited before the Word," says Miss Ridderhof. "I hoped in the Scripture to find some 'out' or else some very clear command to go. But no special message was given me, just the general impact of the Great Commission. I didn't find anything to bolster up my resistance or to urge me forward."

Her promise to God, her realization that "the time is short," and the plain teaching of Scripture caused Joy to accept the appointment of the Friends mission to Honduras.

There her time was indeed short, and opposition faced her at every turn. In a remote hill town she worked with just one Christian companion, an illiterate native girl. The Roman Catholic village priest spared no effort to destroy her work and get rid of the Protestants. Political upheaval, primitive living conditions, and extreme personal danger took their toll. Joy caught a tropical fever.

But how could she leave this little town where she had seen such miracles of grace? She had seen lives transformed by the Gospel. Been rescued again and again from imminent danger. Stood by the death beds of those who had just turned to Christ for salvation. Watched helplessly as young believers were swept away into revolutionary activities. Heard the testimonies of new Christians who blessed God with all the words at their command.

The time was short, the work just beginning. In the excitement of service, Joy hardly realized the condition of her own health.

Back in Los Angeles for a belated furlough, Joy yearned for the needy in the hills of Honduras. A year wasted away and still she lay in her attic room. The tropical disease was stubborn. Seeing no immediate prospect of sending Miss Ridderhof back to the field, the mission board dropped her support. Lying there weak, penniless, with the desire of her heart closed to her, Joy faced what she calls her "rejoicing crisis."

God had been good to her, she reminded herself.

He had lifted from her the burden of a willful temperament. He had given her grace to follow through on her missionary commitment. He had allowed her six intense, fruitful years in Honduras. The way had not been easy, but glory had always followed obedience.

"I at last woke up to the fact that even on my sick bed I must rejoice. God could use me right there in my garret as well as on the mission field. If I would wait, with rejoicing, faith, and expectation, God would work in some greater way to reach the unreached in Honduras."

Thus Gospel Recordings was born. Convalescing, Joy cut a record in Spanish for use back in Honduras. The attic became an office where scripts were prepared. High-fidelity equipment, technical aid, and finances appeared as if on cue.

By the time Joy's health would permit her to go abroad, missionaries to other countries had begun asking for Gospel records. Joy hesitated. How she longed to return to Honduras! But God said to her, "I have other sheep, too, in another fold. I must bring them also . . ." (John 10:16, *Living Gospels*).

Millions around the world had no missionary who knew their language and no Bible to read. Joy promised God that she would make records in any language or dialect for which He would help her find speakers and translators.

Rejoicing as each new door opened, Joy Ridderhof and her team moved forward: to the Navahos first, then the Mexican Indians and the Alaskan Eskimos; to ninety-two Filipino tribal groups, naked Australian aborigines, and on to Ethiopia, the Congo, and the Sudan.

Simple Gospel messages have been recorded in over three thousand languages and new dialects are added each week.

The missionary faith of a girl who has never outgrown being "too impractical" reaches ahead to the day when "every tongue shall confess that Jesus Christ is Lord" (Philippians 2:11).

CHAPTER 8

The Battle of Health

The story begins on the icy plains of central China and concludes in a hospital bed in Shanghai. Between those two points lies a journey of unbelievable drama, danger, and deliverance.

Angel Escort ends with the words, "After a long and hazardous journey we arrived in Shanghai. Soon I was on the operating table while the doctor skillfully removed my troublesome appendix."

During my recuperation I got to know the five-foot, ten-and-a-half-inch, grey-eyed surgeon. Paul Adolph was a doctor totally committed to Christ and to people. Not all who love Christ love people, but Adolph did. His compassion for people sprang from his love for Christ. Paul Adolph, like his Lord, was concerned about the whole man.

The busy doctor provided me the ultimate in comfort and care. He also shared with me his daily spiritual discoveries, and I left the hospital a better man.

It seemed natural to find this distinguished-looking doctor in China. All his life aimed in that direction. Before his birth his parents dedicated him to the Lord for the evangelization of China. In November, 1900, the Boxer Rebellion swept China. At China Inland Mission headquarters in Philadelphia, earnest Christians were praying for missionaries in mortal danger. Paul's parents attended the C.I.M. prayer

---

DR. PAUL E. ADOLPH
Missionary doctor under the China Inland Mission
Author and Surgeon

meetings and promised their third son to the work of God in China.

Growing up close to the China Inland Mission American headquarters, Paul and his eldest brother naturally moved toward China. A weekly family discipline kept the boys aware of this great eastern land.

"Every Sunday," Dr. Adolph reminisces, "my parents got out a missionary box. Each member of the family contributed something, according to his age. I started by putting a penny into the box each Sunday. The money helped support a Bible woman in China. At the same time we corresponded with the MacLeods, missionaries who worked with our Bible woman.

"The Scripture says, 'Where your treasure is, there will your heart be also.' So my eyes were cast upon China, with a definite spiritual interest in bringing the Chinese people to a knowledge of Christ."

Adolph's medical career, also, developed as a natural outgrowth of family influences. Both of Paul's older brothers became teachers of medical subjects, William in China and Edward in New York. What could be more obvious than for a boy raised in such an environment to give his life to medical missions?

But I have been telling the story from the outside. From the inside, from Paul's point of view, the way was neither so obvious nor so easy.

His parents did not tell him of their commitment on his behalf. Instead they trusted the Holy Spirit to lead him. And when Paul was fourteen God spoke to him.

"I was listening to an article from *China's Millions*, which my father was reading to the family on a Sunday afternoon, as was his custom. The article, entitled 'Prayer and Pills,' pictured medical missionary work in China. I didn't say anything or make any comment, but the Holy Spirit was speaking to my heart.

"From that session I went right up to my room. The voice of the Lord spoke clear words to my heart. Kneeling by my bed, I promised God that I would become a medical missionary to China if He would open the way."

Amazingly simple and clear direction! Still, during his years of education, Paul turned this way and that.

A classical education in high school led to a Greek major in college. Should he drop Greek and prepare for medical school? At the end of his junior year at Wheaton College, young Adolph poured out his uncertainties to his Greek professor. Instead of trying to keep the bright student in his department, the professor encouraged Paul to follow God's call into medicine. Paul graduated with double majors, chemistry and Greek, then headed for medical school at the University of Pennsylvania.

Right at this point another detour loomed up. Adolph became deeply interested in Africa. He wrote to Dr. Stirrett of the Sudan Interior Mission. Dr. Stirrett replied negatively. Adolph's dubious health made him a poor risk for an African mission station. The letter to Paul carried the ominous sound of a rusty door slamming shut.

"Only a few weeks later," says Dr. Adolph, "a friend suggested that I visit Dr. Glover, the Home Director of the China Inland Mission. 'Dr. Glover has a real fund of information about all mission fields,' I was told. I found myself calling Dr. Glover on the phone.

"No sooner had I hung up, having made the appointment, than a voice spoke to my heart, 'This means China. You are going to see Dr. Glover. This means China.' I obeyed this inner conviction and applied to the China Inland Mission."

China and medicine—the matter seemed settled. But during his year of internship, an attractive position threatened to derail the young doctor. President Bushwell of Wheaton College invited Paul back to his Alma Mater as college physician and head of the biology department. Delighted with the prospect, Adolph mentioned it to some of the hospital staff. One of the social workers, a former missionary, drew him aside in the corridor.

"She warned me against letting my eyes be turned

away from the mission field," Adolph recalls. "It was once more the Lord speaking to me, I am sure."

Don't you wish God's ways were as clear to you, the detours so easily avoided? A voice in your ear . . . a word when you turned to the right or left?

Dr. Adolph believes that God gives His guidance to those who are willing to obey: "I think it was that strict obedience inculcated in me by my parents that taught me to obey the Lord when He showed me His will."

Often God's Word will come through one of His children—a Greek professor's advice, a staff worker's warning, the chance suggestion of a friend, the negative letter of a senior medical missionary on the field in Africa. The Christian must be willing to submit to the counseling of his fellow Christians, for God intends that His children depend upon one another.

Step by step God used His servants, His still small Voice, and His Word to show Paul Adolph His will and to prevent his being sidetracked. Confident of his Lord's direction for his life, Paul continued his preparations for China.

Then a serious obstacle developed. About four months before he was due to graduate from medical school Adolph contracted pulmonary tuberculosis. Three decades ago treatment was largely a matter of living and sleeping outdoors, graded increases in exercise and plenty of rest. The young intern went through eight months of rigid treatment followed by six months as a part-time staff member of the first tuberculosis sanatorium established in the United States.

His fellow students came to his room to commiserate him. Some grieved at the apparent end of a promising career. Others, who knew of his determination to go to China, scoffed like Joseph's brothers, saying, "Now we shall see what becomes of his dreams!"

Still Paul had the Lord's Word and the help of Christian friends to keep him true to his calling. "I encouraged myself in the Lord, and the Lord's people encouraged me also," was Dr. Adolph's reply to my questions about his recovery. "I remember particularly a medical missionary whom I met at Trudeau Sanatorium. By this time I was recovering and had been assigned the care of several patients. To a medical missionary I gave pneumothorax treatments, injecting air into his pleural cavity. In return, he gave me spiritual shots, putting new hope into my deflated dreams."

Medicine, rest, and prayer restored Adolph's health. But what mission would accept him with T.B. on his record? Missions then and now are very sticky on a candidate's health. A strong, healthy body is a minimal requirement for the rigors of foreign service.

The China Inland Mission required that candidates secure health authorization from a reputable doctor. The assistant director of Trudeau Sanatorium told the C.I.M. Board unofficially that he thought it would be all right for Paul to go abroad. But the sanatorium director was appalled at the idea. Waiting upon God, the mission leaders decided to admit Paul Adolph anyway. His guidance to China was undeniable, and he had an older brother in China to accept family responsibility if Paul should have a relapse.

Some folks thought Paul Adolph was crazy . . . *in his condition*, heading for the rigors of inland China? . . . wasting his life abroad, when physically lesstaxing and intellectually-exciting jobs awaited him in the States?

All they said might be true but Dr. Adolph did not see it that way. He was confident China was God's place for him.

What did he find when he got to China? He found a lovely lassie of Scotch descent by the name of Vivian MacDougall. Though Paul and Vivian had met at the China Inland Mission headquarters in Philadelphia, their romance blossomed during a conference their first summer together in China. A year later they married in Peking. Paul's elder brother, William, opened his home on the Yenching University campus for a delightful wedding reception.

In 1931 the young doctor was designated to the Wilmay Memorial Hospital which had been built back in 1913. This hospital in Luan, Shansi, had been vacant since 1915—the very year the Lord spoke to Paul as a high school freshman kneeling by his bed.

"The hospital had been waiting for me all those years," says Adolph, his kindly grey eyes sparkling. "What a challenge! I sometimes shudder to think how I might have missed the Lord's call to me. God brought great blessing because I obeyed Him and went to the place He had prepared for me since my youth.

"Luan was a major trouble spot during the Boxer Rebellion. Here C.I.M. missionaries were harassed and persecuted. The suffering of those missionaries moved my parents to dedicate me to the work of God in China, and here was the hospital, an opening held for me by the Lord right in the center of former rebel territory. It was a source of real encouragement and joy to me to see the prejudice of hearts broken down by our medical work.

"During the Sino-Japanese War our hospital was filled with war casualties. The wounded came to us across rugged mountains by mule litter, muleback and on foot. A Chinese private with his right knee laid open by a high explosive illustrates my point about prejudice. Maggots crawled in and out of his undressed wound. His fever ran dangerously high. I told him we would give him a blood transfusion and then amputate the leg.

"When I contacted his commanding officer for a blood donor the response was, 'He is only a private. We can't afford blood for him.' Meanwhile in the ward the dying soldier lost no opportunity to revile the staff. The patient gave me the same rude treatment.

"Our entire Chinese and foreign staff responded by praying for the soldier. At this juncture, our head male nurse volunteered to give his blood. As the soldier recovered he questioned why the male nurse would give him blood when the army for which he so bravely fought would not. This must be the love of Christ. From this point on there was no more prejudice. He drank in the Gospel message and his life was suddenly transformed. This loving deed of the male nurse made the Gospel real—irresistible."

Jesus Christ both preached and healed the sick. Deeds added dimension to words. Though terribly busy Jesus was never frustrated. As hospital superintendent, medical administrator, preacher, and surgeon, Adolph too was busy. An accomplished Chinese speaker, he was in constant demand.

Early in his career Adolph concluded that there was always time to do everything God wanted him to do. "God showed me that I could glorify Him as much in removing the inflamed appendix of one of His servants as in preaching a sermon. If my skill was needed for the relief of suffering, that held priority."

From a tuberculosis sanatorium in New York to a hospital in Northwest China is a long way. For Paul Adolph it was a road paved with proof that a life which counts is one that refuses to digress or deviate from the will of God.

CHAPTER 9

Locked Out but Climbing

Easy for Jim Cook to be a missionary? Sure! Long before the boy learned English he chattered in the native dialects of Assam, in Northeastern India.

Assam—land of dense jungles filled with wild animals and wild people. Jim loved the excitement of both. Eager for adventure, careless in the face of danger, the growing boy roamed the hillsides and stream-gutted canyons.

As a lad, Jim frequently trekked into the villages and towns with his missionary father. While Dr. Cook preached, young Jim passed out tracts in the teeming market places. Jim's quick eyes caught the difference between those who knew Christ and those who were without Him. Peace, joy, purpose distinguished the Christians, while their heathen neighbors looked restless, lost. Slowly he came to feel that no adventure could compare with telling people of the reality of Christ.

One special journey inerasably impressed the boy. Dr. Cook took his son from the Upper Assam area to the city of Calcutta. Drought and famine had devastated the region along their route. Jim had never seen so many people—men, women, and children by the thousands.

In Calcutta, father and son forced their way

JIM COOK
Missionary to the Philippines,
Ceylon, and Hawaii under the
Conservative Baptist Foreign Mission Society

through hordes of starving people. From every direction pitiful wails for food assailed them. Overwhelmed, little Jim sobbed convulsively.

Dr. Cook squeezed the boy's hand a little tighter. "Son," he said gently, "take a long look and never forget this awful sight. There is only one thing more terrible—men and women starving for want of Jesus Christ, the Bread of Life."

Jim rubbed his wet face on his daddy's coat sleeve. He determined that when he grew up he would be a missionary and return to India.

With the outbreak of World War II, Jim came to the States to finish his high school education at Lake Crystal, Minnesota. Jim threw himself into the U.S. high school environment with great enthusiasm. The broad-shouldered lad from India had an agile mind, strong coordinated muscles, and the versatility that makes a top athlete. Sharp-eyed coaches soon had the husky missionary kid in uniform most of the year around.

Arriving on the campus of Northwestern College in Minneapolis, Jim turned out for basketball practice. The varsity squad snapped him up, and for four years lanky Cook piled up points. Even theological studies did not prevent him from playing in the Portland Metropolitan League, where he was high scorer in the years 1954 and 1955.

Athletic success brought offers of fame and fortune. Jim confesses, "For a time sports took my eyes off the foreign field. Basketball was a very important part of my life. Interesting opportunities and financial offers bounced my way—tempting sideroads that would have bypassed God's will for me."

While still in college, Jim fell in love and married pretty Sylvia. Soon the difficulties of earning a living, keeping out of debt, and making good college grades piled upon him. As occasions to make money knocked at his door, Jim found it easy, as he says, "to rationalize it into the will of God for my life. I now began to have problems about obedience to the command of Christ. By buying up the opportunities, I reasoned, I could get out of debt and promote the work of the Lord. If God prospered me, I could help support someone else."

Jim recalls another opportunity that came close to sidetracking him: "To make ends meet I was working on a tug boat. In an emergency, with quick thinking and alert action, spiced with a shake of courage, I saved a tug boat from sinking. As a reward, the company made me captain of the boat. Now for the first time I had more money than I needed. Was this not God's special blessing? Now I could help send someone else."

Jim admits that such logic did not quiet his conscience: "Deep within myself I knew God wanted *me*, not a substitute. He wanted me, not my money. How could I cruise along on a frontage road when God wanted me on His freeway? And I surrendered again to the will of God."

Now came a test from a totally unexpected source. During part of Jim's seminary training he served as youth pastor of the large Hinson Memorial Baptist Church in Portland, Oregon.

"It's just not right for Mr. Cook to go to a foreign land and waste such fine preaching on ignorant people," whispered Mr. X.

"Our young people need the bright leadership and attractive personality of Jim Cook," agreed Deacon Y. "Besides who else could coach the church league?"

"I know Mr. Cook plans on foreign service, but he should realize that if he will stay and work with our young people many of them may end up on the foreign field," chimed in Mrs. Z.

Soon Jim found himself responding to the soft-spoken suggestions. Yes, he could serve as a recruiting sergeant in God's army. "But," says Jim, "the Spirit of God gave me the answer. He showed me that God must have my obedience—my life." Jim immediately applied for foreign service.

Even this new obedience didn't bring him entirely out of the woods. His obedience was first severely tested. Since he had grown up in India, he applied to a mission which accepted him for service in that land. But when the Indian government received Cook's visa application, they turned it down. The turndown shocked the young candidate.

"Lord, this doesn't make sense," Jim said. "I

know a number of the languages of India. I know the people and now I can't go."

In church after church he had told the people that the Lord had called him to India. Now what would he say? Unwilling to accept defeat, Jim sent in a second visa request. Its refusal put a night latch on a door already locked. And what did Jim learn from his disappointments?

"Lesson Number One," says Jim. "God does not always let us go the way that seems reasonable and logical. He expects us to walk in obedience and by faith.

"Lesson Number Two. I am called to Christ, not to a people or a country. As my Lord, He has every right to close one door and open another."

The Cooks had made two good tries to get into foreign service. Did the closed door indicate that God wanted them to stay in America? Did they now have an excuse to turn their backs on the millions in distant lands who have not heard of Christ? Jim and Sylvia did not think so. They applied to go to the Philippines and their visas were granted.

They faithfully served the Lord in the Islands until 1959 when Jim discovered his wife was suffering from a rare blood disease. The family hurried back to the States for expert medical care, but on February 1, 1960, Sylvia went to be with her Lord.

Even in "the valley of the shadow of death" Jim found the grace of God sufficient and the peace of God his strength. At his loved one's funeral he spoke of the reality of the risen Christ.

"I just had to walk an hour at a time," Jim honestly admits, "but with each hour Christ was my sufficiency."

Now should Jim give up and stay home? What about his two boys, Jimmy, four, and Johnny, two, and their need for a mother? "I knew God wanted me back in the Orient. I committed our problems to an all-knowing Heavenly Father." In February, 1961, the Lord provided a new wife and mother as Jim married Shirley Soderholm.

Shortly after the knot was tied, Jim and Shirley set sail for Ceylon. Soon after their arrival at Colombo, the capital city, a group of university basketball players came to the Cook home to ask if Jim would coach their team. Cook made the boys a bargain, "If I give my time to coach you fellows, I will expect you to give me your time to come and hear me preach on Sunday." The athletes accepted the deal and kept their promise.

Cook demanded discipline, hard work, and real team play of his players. Soon his team was winning games and other teams were copying their plays and strategy.

Jim really worked at living the Christian life on the pagan campus. Ardent Buddhists and hard-core Communists watched for any slip he might make. Two of Jim's team accepted Christ. Winning games . . . winning youth . . . Jim did both.

But the opportunity that thrilled Jim distressed the head Buddhist priest at the university. Jealous religious leaders, enraged by Jim's popularity, manufactured lies and rumors about the young coach. Ambiguous tales devoid of fact suggested that the Cooks were not good for the university . . . not good for Ceylon. The Cooks were told to go.

Will the Cooks give up now, find a U.S. pastorate safe from sudden illness and fierce heathen persecution? No! They are gone again, this time to the Hawaiian Islands.

Adventure? What challenge could compare with that of bringing Jesus Christ's redeeming love to men who have not heard? What triumph could be more thrilling than to watch men open their hearts and minds to the Savior?

CHAPTER 10

A Split-Level Home—
A High-Powered Car

"Only one thing has led me and kept me on the mission field—the will of God." In these honest, forceful words, Dr. Donald E. Hoke, president of Japan Christian College, summarizes his reason for being in Japan.

The romance of living in an exotic Asiatic country means nothing to this man of action. God's leading in his life, he states, has been "the clear command of Christ and my obedience to it."

Don vividly remembers a period of spiritual conviction in his twelfth year of life. Going into his parents' bedroom, after they had retired, he asked them how he could be saved. At their instructions he knelt by their bedside and prayed, asking Christ to save him and come into his heart.

Even so, he went into high school with no apparent change in his life. He would argue vehemently concerning the truth of the Bible with an atheistic English teacher but would go out of the classroom to live and talk exactly like the rest of the students.

"At that time," he recalls, "I didn't know a single evangelical Christian."

Don's parents were good church members. Born

DR. DONALD E. HOKE
Missionary to Japan under
The Evangelical Alliance Mission
President of Japan Christian College

in Chicago, he was reared in what everyone called a fine Christian home. Father and mother faithfully attended the Methodist church in Park Ridge, and his father became a steward and financial secretary in the church. Mr. Hoke was a man who lived a very clean, fine moral life. Only one thing was lacking —he had never been converted.

One day he stopped at the theater meeting conducted by the Chicago Christian Business Men's Committee to encourage them in their work. He heard Dr. William McCarrell speak bluntly and pointedly on the need of the new birth and, at the age of 55, young Don's father was converted.

Through a series of circumstances, his parents placed Don in Wheaton Academy for his senior year in high school. Their desire was to remove Don from the influences of certain of his closest friends.

"Thinking back on that move," he says, "I went with teeth gritted, determined that I would not conform to the Christian ideals there and having made a bargain with my parents that at the end of that year I could go to the secular university of my choice to study law. But in February of that year, at the regular semester evangelistic services of the college in which the Academy students participated, *God met me.*"

This time his conversion was real, but let him tell his own story:

"After hearing Dr. Robert C. McQuilkin speak all week I remember vividly the closing Friday night service. I sat at the right rear of the auditorium. He was speaking on Romans 12:1, 2. Finally the time for decisions came. I sat there gripping the back of the seat in front of me, as he presented the claims of Christ on my body. Finally, after an internal struggle, realizing what I would have to give up—my old friends, my ambitions, my hopes—I stood quietly and unemotionally, committing my life to Christ to do His will. I then thought I was 'surrendering' to Christ. I now believe this was the time of my true conversion."

By this time the family had moved to a more evangelical church. Any strength Don had wasted in restless rebellion he now put into active service in the Baptist church in Oak Park. Following graduation from the Academy he enrolled as a freshman at Wheaton College.

Now began a spiritual revolution. His earliest ambition was to become a prosperous Christian businessman, making a great deal of money. With this he would send many young people to the mission field, while he lived in comparative sacrifice in a split-level home in suburbia with two handsome high-powered cars in the garage.

That first year he majored in economics. But through the regular chapel services and a work of God in his heart he slowly began to doubt that this was the will of God for his life.

During his sophomore year, God sent Dr. James R. Graham, a dynamic missionary from China, to the campus. Though the class he was teaching was Bible survey, every day God's claim on Don's life for world evangelism was driven home. This only increased the spiritual struggle in Don's heart. During this year he decided on a compromise course. He would be neither a businessman nor a missionary. He would be a pastor and send many young people from his church to the mission field.

Having settled that, he now waited for the spiritual unrest in his heart to quiet, but found it impossible to throw off the lingering misgiving that the pastorate was not the will of God for him.

"Finally," he recalls, "during the second semester of my sophomore year the conviction grew upon me that the command of Jesus Christ to 'go into all the world and preach the Gospel to every creature' demanded my obedience. There was no way of escaping the irresistible logic of the command. I had no excuse to offer and no reason to stay home. I could not find refuge in any other Scripture. It seemed to me as a normal, healthy, and able young Christian I had to consider *first* the command of Jesus Christ to take the Gospel where Christ had not been named."

This conviction climaxed in a decision at the semester's evangelistic meeting at Wheaton College in February of his sophomore year. When the invitation was given for those who would follow Christ in missionary service, he arose and stood with scores of others. Even the girl with whom he was keeping company was pushed into the background of his mind. Here was a responsibility to God to which he must respond . . . to which he must give first place.

From this decision the point of Don's compass was set and he did not waver. He had made a deep and resolute purpose to become a foreign missionary simply on the basis of the command of Jesus Christ. Upon graduation from college Don went east for a change of viewpoint during the summer months and spent much time praying about what graduate school or seminary he should attend.

During that time a new church started by six laymen in the very town in which he had been reared was organized. Because Don had worked his way through college as a newspaper reporter, they asked him to write the publicity to attract attention to the new church for the two weekly local papers during the summer. He faithfully mailed the news releases back from the East.

"Probably out of courtesy," Don says, "that fall the leaders of the church asked me to preach for a month on my return."

The invitation seemed to confirm his guidance to continue his studies at the Wheaton College Graduate School of Theology. At the end of the first month of preaching, the deacons asked Don to become the pastor of the small new church, which was then meeting in a field house. For six years he stayed, seeing the erection of the first building debt free, laying the foundation of a missionary program, and completing his graduate work at the same time.

During his third year as pastor of the church a young undergraduate of Wheaton College came out to sing. Don was immediately attracted to Martha Cowman, "not only by her lovely singing voice but by her vivacious personality." For some time the courtship seemed to be unsteady, perhaps because she did not understand that Don was a missionary volunteer. As a high school student, she had committed her life to Christ for foreign service under Dr. Robert McQuilkin.

When Martha finally learned that Don, too, had given his life for foreign service, she consented to become his wife. As man and wife, for more than two years they continued in the happy ministry of the little community church at Park Ridge.

Both Don and Martha, though happy in their service, sensed an unrest and knew they had to step out toward the mission field. But where and when did He want them to go? Dr. McQuilkin came to their church to hold meetings one weekend and as a result invited Don to become his assistant in the ministry at Columbia Bible College.

The first thought that came to Don's heart was, "Is this a stumbling block to keep us from the mission field?"

After a year of prayer the Hokes decided that Columbia Bible College with its vital missionary program was probably a stepping-stone to the mission field. So in 1947 they resigned their church, and he began five happy years as Assistant to the President of Columbia Bible College.

As those years came to a close, once again Don and Martha sensed an unrest. In spite of the fact that Dr. McQuilkin was not well and was leaning more heavily upon Don for assistance, God's command in years past rose again. So together they began to pray definitely that by January 31, 1951, God would guide to the field and to the mission under which they should serve.

They prayed earnestly, but January 31 came and went and there seemed to be no guidance. Yet they could not feel that this was God's hand guiding them to stay home. Then one day a friend from Japan visited them. He suggested that though China was closed, for he knew of their interest in China, they should go to Japan under The Evangelical Alliance Mission.

Don had previously made a survey trip of that field and knew something of the opportunity and open door in Japan. So Don and his wife began to pray earnestly about it. But there was no vision, no voice from heaven, and no external guidance. Little by little the conviction formed, however, that this might well be the leading of God.

Don records a most practical incident in their going to the field:

"We prayed for the $100 necessary to go to the Annual Conference of T.E.A.M. in Chicago. The date was mid-May, 1052. Again our self-imposed deadline for the travel funds came and went with no money. But a couple of days later the Board of Trustees of Columbia Bible College, at the instigation of Dr. McQuilkin, granted me enough money as a gift to attend the conference. In faith Martha and I went. The mission board examined and accepted us for service in Japan. This confirmed our guidance."

Now things began to move quickly. They prayed, planned, and sent a letter to their friends. On June 16 their house was sold. On July 15 their baggage was shipped. By the grace and leading of God, all support was pledged, passage and equipment funds were in, and they were ready to go in September of that year. Even a shipping strike on the West Coast did not stop them. On a business trip to New York, by faith Don booked passage on a passenger vessel and by October, 1952, the Hoke family was in Japan.

Since 1952, they have served under T.E.A.M. in Japan. For the past fifteen years Don has been President of Japan Christian College, an outstanding school founded to train Japanese Christians for positions of leadership as pastors, evangelists, and teachers in the national church. God is blessing the school and there are now over 250 alumni, some seventy-five percent of whom are serving Christ, not only in Japan but in other parts of Asia and the world.

One has to go below the surface to find things that might have kept Don from foreign service. Here is a man with a natural inclination, interest and talents in the area of business and with a desire to make money and to have things. The pull of materialism constituted a real struggle.

Even God's blessing upon his pastorate experience became a subtle temptation. For long months he struggled with the idea of turning aside from missionary service. After all, was not God using him where he was? Could he not serve the Lord in this way and be a "sending station" for many other young people? Could he not justify himself in both his usefulness and fruitfulness by staying at home?

His years of teaching at Columbia Bible College seemed to strengthen this logic. "Think," he would say to himself, "of the tremendous number of young people who will go into foreign service from Columbia Bible College, and I am having a part in sending them out. This is my area of usefulness. In this way I can multiply myself around the world." Very true—but for Don at least it was not the will of God.

What is it that has kept the Hokes in foreign service, even in times of pressure, frustration, and discouragement in Japan? Dr. Hoke has an answer to that question:

"The simple command of Christ, 'Go,' is enough for me. I have found no excuse for turning aside from His divine imperative. It has not always been easy. The fact that my wife has been a partner with me in the commitment a hundred percent, that she herself was a missionary volunteer of unswerving purpose before I met her, has been a tremendously helpful factor. But, supremely, God's leading in my life has simply been the clear command of Jesus Christ and my obedience to it."

CHAPTER 11

"The Battle of the Talented"

"Singing Ambassador" is no mere public relations title for Norman Nelson. He has sung in vast arenas and in the private chambers of presidents. His powerful tenor voice has filled the public squares of towns and hamlets in a dozen outlands.

He has sung in person before audiences totaling more than three million in the Orient, and his magnificent tenor voice is recognized and loved by thousands more who hear him daily on the radio.

"We are Christ's ambassadors," is the message of Norm's songs. "God is using us to speak to you: we beg you, as though Christ Himself were here pleading with you, receive the love He offers you" (II Corinthians 5:20, *Living Letters*). And the vibrant operatic tenor rolls forth a verse of "There Is No Greater Love" or "It's Real, I Know It's Real."

Testimonies to the reconciling work accomplished in the hearts of many listeners fill Norm's mail box. "I will always thank and praise God for sending you to Davao City," writes a Filipino girl. "You know, sir, every member of my family received the Lord through the message in your wonderful songs."

Norm's own life was transformed by the message

NORMAN NELSON
Missionary with Overseas Crusades
Tenor Soloist
Singing Ambassador-at-Large
Overseas Crusades Board Member

of a song, one which he himself was singing. Singing was the thing he liked best to do as a child, and Sunday school and church provided him with an abundant repertoire. He was singing to himself one day when he realized that the words of the chorus were meant for him. "Come into my heart, Lord Jesus," he sang, making it his own prayer and in that instant receiving new life as a son of God.

Since the age of thirteen, then, Norm has belonged to God, but throughout his high school and college days again and again he faced the question of how best to use his growing talent. As a result of Norm's excellent portrayal of Faust in a high school performance of Verdi's Opera, his music teacher offered him a scholarship to study for a career in opera. Norm was already being coached by the leading operatic tenor in Denver and was invited to audition for the Jack Benny show. With his dynamic voice and winning stage presence, Norm was a natural for a career in professional entertainment.

But once again a song gripped his heart and transposed his life. One Sunday evening as a college quartet sang at his church, Norm heard God's call to full-time Christian service and vowed to use his voice always in consonance with the glory of his Lord. His musical training then took on added seriousness, as he realized that his vocal skill could amplify or deaden the impact of the words he sang.

But the sacrifices were real ones. From the glamor of a professional career, Norm and his pert wife Georgia turned to the hardships of financial and geographical insecurity. Norm worked as Youth for Christ director, as minister of visitation, as singer on evangelistic teams, and as pastor. After over a dozen moves in ten years, the Nelsons and their little children finally settled down in a home which Norm, contrasting it to some of the parsonages and apartments they had known, describes as having "wall-to-wall floors."

At this point God introduced a new theme, running contrary to the growing security of the young pastor. Norm was suddenly confronted by the challenge of missions. Already a dedicated minister, disciplined to a life of sacrificial obedience, surely the decision would be easy for him. But no. He faced several real obstacles.

The first was ignorance. Let Norm make his own confession:

"At best I had a distorted picture of missionaries and missions in general. Although I had pastored two different churches, missions to me was a charitable enterprise to which we donated our funds each year. And to be truthful, our incentive in giving to missions was the desire to be up towards the top in our district as a church. Since none of the other churches did very much for missions, we were third or fourth from the top, although we gave only $1,200 a year from a church with 250 active members."

In the summer of 1955, a trip to the Orient opened Norm's eyes. With an evangelist and chalk artist, he toured Japan, Formosa, and the Philippines, singing in school assemblies, village plazas, and city auditoriums. People by the thousands came to listen, particularly in the Philippines, where the cordial American with his resonant voice was an immediate hit. The impact of his singing, coupled with the genuine and eager response of the people to the Gospel, woke Norm up.

Scenes from the tour nagged Norm that fall. Should he continue a ministry in the States when such an arpeggio of opportunity awaited in the Orient? When he received an invitation from Overseas Crusades to serve in the Philippines for two years, Norm took it as God's downbeat. But there was a second snag.

Georgia Nelson had not gone on that summer tour. She had stayed in America expecting their fourth child and, for the first time in ten years, enjoying a measure of security. Norm had a good position in a fine church, with invitations to sing almost every evening throughout the Los Angeles area. They had purchased a home of their own, and some of the furniture was already paid for. They had even arranged financing for a brand new automobile after years of struggling with mechanical has-beens.

"Could God really ask them to break up housekeeping and start all over again?" Georgia wondered.

Knowing feminine psychology, Norm soon capitulated to his wife's arguments, saying soothingly, "Honey, you are absolutely right. This measure of security is God's gift to us. We should be grateful for it and not even consider leaving it to go to the mission field."

"Now wait a minute," Georgia objected, and gave her husband a little sermon about the importance of obeying God no matter what the cost.

For two days Norm played obstinate. As he tells the story, "Georgia preached to me with such fervor during those two days that she herself was convinced without a shadow of a doubt that this was what God wanted for us." With a roguish grin he adds, "You should have seen the mixture of triumph and vexation on her face when I told her I'd been determined to go all along!"

Once their hearts were in tune with each other and with God's will, Norm and Georgia's material ties unraveled more easily than they had imagined.

"It is amazing," says Norm, "How the things that seem so precious to you can suddenly become so much excess baggage. Believe it or not, we were thrilled when finally the real estate man told us the house was sold. We were able to sell all our furniture and get rid of our car. Within three months we had been given a new station wagon for our work on the field, our support and passage money was raised and we were ready to go."

Oh, the thrill of using a God-given talent to its full capacity . . . the delight of singing the Gospel to eager, attentive crowds . . . the deep satisfaction of following up genuine conversions. Norm and Georgia had known nothing like it in their American ministry.

Norm teamed up with Filipino evangelist Greg Tingson and began a crusade ministry that saw over thirty thousand respond to Gospel invitations during Nelson's first four years in the Philippines.

"We met in the plaza of one Muslim community," writes Norm, describing a typical meeting. "As the evening service began we stood on the makeshift platform. First of all, I gave a concert. Then Greg

Tingson preached a dynamic Gospel message. Rarely have I seen a more attentive audience.

"In this Muslim area where during an entire campaign usually only one or two will care to publicly acknowledge Christ as Savior, we were astonished to see thirty step forward. To some of these it will mean persecution, being disowned by their families, and even the threat of death."

But it takes more than an overseas location to make a missionary . . . more than a charming cordiality and a magnetic voice. The missing ingredient was one which Norman Nelson sought for a long time.

"I didn't have a burden for the lost," he admits. "I didn't love my neighbor. I didn't have a real desire to see him won. I prayed for this love. I tried in many ways to gain the same burden for souls that caused John Knox to cry, 'Give me Scotland or I die.' Yet I had to be honest with myself: the concern just wasn't there. What was wrong with me? I prayed. I read my Bible. I tried and tried.

"Then God spoke to me through Romans 6:13. I realized that in order to have a burden for the lost I would have to see them through God's eyes, not through my own. 'Yield your members as instruments of righteousness unto God.' Surely an instrument does not try to play itself. As long as I tried to drum up my own emotions I was out of step with God. But when I yielded myself as an instrument God produced His own harmony."

"If you want a burden for the lost," says Norm from his own experience, "if you want to become a missionary, allow God to make you His own instrument. God's eyes see each man compassionately, knowing and hating his sinfulness, but providing and desiring his salvation. When I become God's tool, I no longer see my neighbor through self-centered eyes, but I see him as God sees him—with a redemptive purpose in mind.

"Now as I stand in the market place of an Oriental town, absorbing the unique sights and smells and sounds, there is a deep compassion within my heart.

I look out on a plaza filled with sinful human beings, whose hearts know fear and failure, guilt and grief, and I feel something of what Jesus must have felt as He looked over the city of Jerusalem and cried, 'How often I have wanted to gather your children together' (Matthew 23:37, *Living Gospels*)."

Another obstacle Norm faced he named "the battle of the talented." But God gave him grace to play the right chord.

"If God will not share His glory with another," says Norm, "then God and I will not get glory from the same performance. I soon learned that you cannot at one and the same time show how great you are and how wonderful your Lord is. The choice is not a once-for-all proposition, but rather a day-by-day experience. Each day I simply ask God to let me sing for *His* glory."

Norm admits that even after becoming a foreign missionary he had his problems, the toughest one being the inferiority complex he developed about being "just a missionary." Like most missionaries Norm finds it necessary to travel a great deal. So now we see him on a sleek jet liner. Seated next to him is a sharp up-and-coming young executive. Soon they are in conversation.

After the young businessman has explained his work, he turns to Norm and says, "And, by the way, what's your line?"

"I would put on my best smile," Norm says, "look him right in the eye, and reply, 'I'm a missionary.' Suddenly a startled expression would come across his face. I could almost hear the wheels turning in his mind as he said to himself, "Oh, no, a real live one right here beside me.' Then an amazing transformation would take place. The stark expression of amazement would change to a far-off, visionary expression and, looking out into space, he would say in a pious tone, 'My, that's a wonderful calling!'

"He didn't mean a word of it. It was a poor cover up. All the time he was thinking, 'This poor monk, living off the hills, doesn't know what life is all about.' After many such encounters a mounting inferiority complex began to build in my mind and I would say to myself, 'This man is in big business, but I am just a missionary!'"

I am going to let Norm tell you how God took care of this problem: "One of my missionary journeys took me to M'Lang, Cotabato, on the island of Mindanao in the Philippines. This is a pioneer town, much like in the days of the Old West here in the United States. The people are homesteaders who have come from everywhere in the Philippines. The roads are dust or mud, depending on the weather.

"We met out in an open field where they had just completed a new bandstand. This was to be the site of the town plaza—some mañana. Prior to the meetings the sound truck went through the city, blaring the news that an Americano tenor would be giving a concert in the plaza. The people love singing, and they came by the hundreds.

"One little light bulb hung over my head as I sang. This one hundred-watt illumination dwindled to fifty watts by the time the other lights in the town went on, and every insect for miles around decided that it was convention time in the plaza. Around and around the bulb they flew—crawling in my hair, in my eyes, up my nose, on my ears, and down my shirt. There had been a time when I was so fearful of insects that with one fly in the air while I sang I would inhale each quick breath with dread. Now, during every song, they would fly in and out of my mouth—some to be inhaled, never to be seen again, and others to be spat out with my consonants. It was quite a choice. I never knew whether to swallow or spit.

"As I sat on the platform, discouraged with all of this, I thought, 'What if some fanatic out there would take a shot at us through the darkness? They would just dig a hole and say, "There lies another missionary." There isn't much notoriety in this. What am I doing out here anyway?'

"Then by His Holy Spirit, God began to move on the hearts of the people as Greg preached and I sang. Attitudes changed. Decisions were made. During the week more than three hundred in that little town had acknowledged their need of Christ. By the end of the week, sixty were ready for baptism. On the final Sunday morning they stood with radiant faces, giving witness before the people of the town to their faith in Jesus Christ as Lord and Savior.

"As I sat in that two-hour-long baptismal service, God seemed to thunder the words to my heart and mind, 'THIS IS BIG BUSINESS!' There is nothing more important than the transformation of a life. People are more important than position, popularity, or wealth. What kind of a job—if it paid $1,000 a week—or a performance could possibly compare with this?

"Now when I face a businessman and he says, 'And, by the way, what's your line?' I respond, 'I am a missionary. And that is the biggest business in the world!' And if he is not convinced when I am through with him, at least he is convinced that I am convinced!"

CHAPTER 12

Sick but Obedient

Consumption—tuberculosis in our language—was a killer at the turn of the century. Early or late, it marked its victims with pallor, lassitude, and a racking cough.

In China, hard work in damp weather on inadequate food left millions of people easy prey to the debilitating disease. Missionaries kept on the alert for early symptoms, so that complete rest and a change of climate could be arranged in time to spare their lives.

Evangelistic work is hard on the respiratory system. I should know. My first assignment in China stood me in market squares for hours, preaching at the top of my lungs to interested but far from silent crowds. Meals were noodles sometimes garnished with soybeans, peanuts or hot peppers—hardly a diet calculated to soothe the throat. From one meeting to another I bicycled, as much as sixty miles a day, in and out of cloudbursts.

As for climate, in China one has a choice between the arid lands of the north with their near-Siberian winters and the warm monsoon lands of the south where summers are muggy and winters are moldy-moist. No, I would not recommend China as a mission field for anyone with tuberculosis.

WILLIAM ENGLUND
Missionary to China under
The Evangelical Alliance Mission
Author of Chinese Commentaries

Pioneer evangelist William Englund was not yet twenty when he noticed his breath beginning to come short in the icy Minnesota winters. Speaking to a gathering of Christians in a rough spruce cabin, he lost his voice. At the next homestead where he preached he had to call for water to stop a spell of hoarse coughing.

Tuberculosis was the doctor's diagnosis. And his prescription: seek a milder climate.

To William the verdict struck a double blow. Evangelism was his calling. And of all the organs, an evangelist needs hearty lungs and larynx. Would consumption mean the end of William's ministry?

Young Englund's evangelistic career had begun when he was just twelve years old. His first audiences were unresponsive—not one hand raised or an "Amen" whispered. But they listened quietly, seemed contented, and thoughtfully chewed their cuds during the sermons.

A herd of Holsteins heard William's first attempts at Bible exposition. The boy drove the family cattle to open meadows each summer morning, watched them all day, and herded them back to the barn at night. In his pocket the lively cowherd carried a small Swedish Bible. As the cows grazed, William read and pondered. By noon, when the cattle lay down together in a cool place to rest, the budding preacher would have his text prepared and be ready to expound to his captive congregations the truths he had discovered.

Before long William's parents became aware of their son's enthusiasm. They provided him chances to give his testimony and occasionally to speak at one of the rural church services. When he was sixteen they released him from farm duties for an eight-month Bible school course, the boy's only formal training beyond the sixth reader. Bible school prepared William for itinerant evangelism in the scattered homesteads of Minnesota.

For two winters young Englund threw himself into the work of rural preaching. Traveling by horse, foot, or oxcart from one settlement to another. Conducting meetings. Organizing and encouraging isolated churches. Battling blizzards and facing days of deep freeze. Helping chop wood here, mend a roof there. Bringing the Good News of the Gospel to the newcomers who poured in from Norway and Sweden at the turn of the century.

Now the dread word "consumption" crashed down to bar the energetic young Swede from the evangelistic work he loved.

In the second place, tuberculosis meant that he must leave his beautiful state of ten thousand lakes. William was born in a borrowed cabin the very first winter his parents moved to Minnesota. They had come from Aland Island in the Gulf of Bothnia, lured by the promise of free land and good farming.

The years had prospered the Englunds. From that first shack—a dirt-floored room with straw thatch and unplastered board walls—they had graduated to a comfortable farm house big enough to serve as a meeting place for the entire community. Hardy Swedes, they had weathered many a sub-zero winter.

But William's illness changed matters and was one of the reasons the Englunds pulled up stakes, auctioned off their goods, and moved to the West Coast.

I would hardly vote for Seattle as an ideal location for consumptives. Though rainy, the Pacific Northwest had mild winters. And the growing Scandinavian community there (at the turn of the century) included friends of the Englunds.

Father soon found work in the shipyards, and William, after a short stint in the furniture business, reached out as an itinerant evangelist in the new settlement areas around Puget Sound.

Sometimes he took a boat or train along the coasts of the great bay. More often he walked, along footpaths through the maritime rain forests, over roughly paved roads between dock workers' shanties. Big black umbrella fending off the pattering rain. Guitar strung over one shoulder. Satchel or clothes and a Bible. High leather boots sloughing up hillocks of mud.

William found plenty of work in the Seattle area. Here too immigrants were lonely, rootless, facing grimly the uncertainties of a new way of life. Englund preached in chapels, workers' halls, living rooms, and newly formed churches much as he had done back in Minnesota. When his breath came short or his voice weakened, he tried to turn his concern into prayer.

By taking care of himself, eating wisely, getting adequate rest, the young man might have many years of rich ministry before him in the States.

But William's friend, Mr. Solomon Bergstrom, had bigger ideas. "Come to China," was Bergstrom's proposal. "I believe God wants you in China. Drop everything and come with us now."

The Bergstroms stayed in the Englund home in Seattle before embarking for China. The families had met in Minnesota where Mr. Bergstrom, China missionary on furlough, had often joined William on his preaching tours. Bergstrom continually urged William to pray for China and consider going as an evangelist.

Another China missionary had held meetings among the scattered congregations in Minnesota. Lena Hedman was a gifted speaker with a reputation for bringing revivals wherever she went. A woman preacher with a name like "head man"? William was rather dubious.

But Lena proved to be a jolly little Swedish dumpling, warmhearted and unassuming, with a round face and a merry laugh. She and William shared several meetings, and she too thrust before him the prospect of mission work in China.

How long would a tubercular preacher last on rice and soybeans? William wondered. When the Bergstroms showed up in Seattle, William put off their insistent demands that he accompany them to the Far East. But he agreed to pray about the possibility of service abroad.

The Bergstroms sailed for China, and William threw himself back into the Seattle work.

Conducting a campaign not far from the city, the young preacher found a prayer place along the river bank in a coppice of alders. Here he prayed each day, not about missions but about his series of meetings.

One afternoon as William prayed, God confronted him with the question of China. "Are you willing to go?" the Lord asked.

Englund hurriedly brought out all his legitimate excuses. He had no formal training—just six years of public school and eight months of Bible school. He had no financial backing. And he was suffering from tuberculosis, for which his generation knew no sure remedy.

"What are your excuses to Me?" the Lord seemed to reply. "Will you obey Me or not?"

William balked. Deep in his heart he was not willing to go. As he puts it, "The real hindrance that held me back was my lack of yielding to the Lord for work on the mission field." The crux of the question was which would come first—God's will or Englund's unwillingness?

You have seen children fuss with their parents over some trifle—putting on shoes or eating pudding. At first Johnny is full of legitimate excuses and mother reasons with him patiently, but soon she realizes that the real conflict is set up by Johnny's sheer irrational obstinacy. Only when he gives in to mommy is she able to go ahead with the meal or the outing or the game which she has planned for Johnny's good.

William Englund finally looked up and prayed, "Lord, I will not hold back. Thy will be done."

At that point he sensed unmistakably that God would send him to China. And the power of Christ was released—odd that our stubbornness can be a hindrance to the Almighty—to begin ironing out the obstacles and smoothing Englund's way to the Far East.

When Lena Hedman came to Seattle in the spring William told her of his commitment and confided his concern over his biggest obstacle to foreign service, his tubercular lungs. He had scarcely enough strength for even the evangelistic services he was then engaged in.

William and Lena decided to fast for a day in order to pray about William's physical condition. They met at dawn in the Christian home where Lena was staying. Alternating hours of prayer with chapters of Bible study, they sought the Lord's treatment for William's disease.

Kneeling by a blue study chair, William prayed, "Lord, You made it clear that I am to go to China. You know I will need lungs capable of standing the strain of the work you have called me to. So I give my weak, sick lungs over to you."

And the Lord literally took the weak lungs, giving Englund complete health in return. From that day on the tuberculosis was miraculously gone. Eventually X-rays were available to confirm, by showing only scars of a former condition, the healing God had performed in answer to prayer.

There is a wonderful power in praying together, and that day of prayer changed William's life in more ways than one.

Lena stayed in Seattle several months, busy in meetings throughout the city. Englund caught himself looking out for her cheery face in the churches which he served. Lena was a good friend of Mrs. Englund's, and what a thumping William's heart would set up when he came home to hear them laughing together in the kitchen!

Why should he be so interested in a lady preacher some seven or eight years his senior? Before many weeks the more pressing question in William's mind was whether she could possibly be interested in him.

When at length he gathered courage to confess his love, William found Lena reluctant on only one point. Could they keep their engagement secret until their current series of meetings was over? Lena was afraid the congregation would be distracted from the messages if they knew about the romance.

What had been Englund's three objections to becoming a missionary?

He had no formal training. No, but he had several years of practical ministry among the settlers of Minnesota and the churches of Seattle. He had the kind of incentive that drove him, on his own, to learn Latin and New Testament Greek. And, when he set out for China at twenty-one years of age he took a companion who already knew the Chinese language and customs. Through her introduction to the people and the work, William adjusted quickly to Oriental life.

He had no financial support. But the churches which he and Lena served rallied quickly to their aid. The congregation of the First Covenant Church in Seattle, where William and Lena were married early in 1903, made their own innovation on the wedding ceremony. They added a missionary service at which gifts were received for the travel and outfitting expenses of the young couple.

He had tuberculosis. Over three score years later Mr. Englund testifies, "If there is anything that I have used as a missionary—especially in my early terms—it has been my lungs. In visiting villages and small towns, sometimes facing thousands gathered out of doors, I spoke morning to night without the aid of a public address system. In spite of the strain, my voice has hardly ever failed. I have felt exhausted, certainly, but my lungs have never given out nor my voice grown hoarse."

God used this man's tireless voice to bring the message of salvation to countless thousands across the farmlands of Shensi.

And what is this grand old missionary doing as I record his story for you? Seated at his desk with his Chinese Bible and his commentaries, he is still busy in the Chinese language. He fills sheet after sheet from right to left with neat columns of Chinese characters. Stone deaf to everything but the Word of God, he records the messages God gives him for the Chinese Christians.

CHAPTER 13

"If You Want to Go to Jail"

As Abe Van Der Puy entered the large red brick building he had no idea that the entire course of his life would be changed within forty-five minutes.

This was Abe's second year at Wheaton College. During his first year he experienced long periods of confusion and restlessness. He kept asking himself, "What is God's plan for my life?"

As the desire to know God's will increased, Abe probed into his commitment to Christ with searching questions. Was he really willing to go any place and do anything for Jesus Christ? What if the Lord wanted him to forget his desire to be a businessman and become a missionary? Abe knew Jesus Christ as a wonderful Savior, but what about this business of discipleship with its evident cost and demand for total obedience?

Earnest bull sessions, and even purposeful times of prayer, seemed nonproductive. But now sophomore Abe sat listening to Dr. Isaac Page, as the missionary pictured a world without Christ. Abe recalls:

"I knew that God was laying His hand upon my shoulder. Every Scripture verse that spoke of taking the Gospel to the lost spoke directly to me. I knew that these commands had a direct personal relationship to my own life. Joyfully, therefore, in the Friday

ABE C. VAN DER PUY
Missionary to Ecuador
President of the
World Radio Missionary Fellowship

91

evening meeting, when the call for missionary volunteers went out, I moved forward while everyone was singing 'Where He leads me I will follow.'

"At the same time, possible service in Latin America loomed very large in my thinking. In testimony of this decision, I immediately obtained a world map and wrote on it, 'God helping me I give myself for Gospel service to reach those who have never heard the message of Jesus Christ.' Alongside this declaration of intent I also wrote Isaiah 6:8.

"From that time on I prepared actively for missionary service. The Lord kept confirming the direction of Latin America to me. I put up another map and encircled the land of Peru to pray especially for that land. I began giving to missions. I concentrated on Spanish language study."

The decision to be a missionary came as a surprise to Abe's family, for as far as you can look back on both sides of the family tree you find none who entered full-time Christian service. Abe's father quite naturally planned for him to join the family business.

Abe entered his world in Sheboygan, Wisconsin, on October 11, 1919. At the time of his birth his father joined his uncle in the purchase of a food store business. They had good success and in 1929, just before the depression broke, formed a company for the manufacture of paper boxes. The depression years were loaded with difficulties. However, both businesses survived the depression.

Although the family never had great material abundance, they did not know as much of shortage and financial difficulties as many did.

Father and Mother Van Der Puy were faithful in taking their two sons and two daughters to church. Prayer before and after meals, Abe remembers, along with reading of the Scriptures, was a part of the tradition of the home. As a boy Abe attended a parochial school maintained by the local Christian Reformed Church.

Though Abe's early home, church, and school life all had a relationship to the Bible, nevertheless, for him much of it had more of external form than internal reality. He tells of his conversion:

"In spite of the fact that I had read the Scriptures many times and that I knew a great deal about Christian doctrine, up until my senior year in high school I could certainly not be called a Christian. Late in my senior year, one Sunday morning, our local pastor made a direct hit on my heart by the power of the Holy Spirit. After the service I went to my room at home and there at my bedside I received Jesus Christ as my personal Savior."

Following this encounter with Christ, Abe became conscious of the directing hand of God upon his shoulder. One day his high school had a college preparation day, when the students were given opportunity to get acquainted with different schools by means of catalogues and other advertising materials.

During the course of the day someone picked up a catalogue from Wheaton College and said to Abe, "Here, take this. If you want to go to jail, this is it."

Since he had just come to know Christ as Savior, this disdainful remark actually whetted Abe's appetite. He took the catalogue home. The phrase, "For Christ and His Kingdom," on the front fascinated this young Christian. Before long he made application to Wheaton and was accepted.

That sophomore year at Wheaton gave direction to Abe's life. During his junior and senior years, he kept the world and its needs constantly before him by participating in the work of the Student Foreign Missionary Fellowship and by active endeavor to witness through a Gospel team.

Following graduation Abe spent two years in Calvin Seminary. His missionary zeal was still evident. When he proposed to Dolores Hicks he told her if she accepted him she must be prepared to be a missionary. Dolores had the same heart for foreign missions, and on June 15, 1943, they were married.

During their two years of seminary, the Van Der Puys pastored the Open Bible Church and did everything possible to emphasize missions. However, in both husband and wife, there was a restlessness and a growing desire to get to the field.

As Paul's arrival in Lystra and his counsel with Timothy was a major factor in that young man's becoming a foreign missionary, so God used the counsel of a busy missionary to further clear Abe's path into foreign service. But let Abe tell it:

"In our second student pastorate, I directed a global missionary conference. One of the missionary speakers was the Reverend Paul Young of the Christian and Missionary Alliance and later of the American Bible Society. I had heard him while a student at Wheaton and was much impressed with him. During the conference he spent quite a few hours in our home.

"At one point, since he knew us pretty well and bearing in mind my wife's singing, etc., he said, 'I believe that God could use you folks at radio station HCJB in Quito, Ecuador.' Later on he said, 'If you will permit me, I would like to get in touch with Clarence Jones and tell him about you.' "

Abe and Dolores gave Mr. Young permission and soon Clarence Jones was in touch with them. They had several conferences. As they prayed and sought the mind of God, more and more it seemed that He was directing them to HCJB. Therefore, they made application, were accepted, and in October, 1945, went to Quito, Ecuador.

Abe honestly admits there were pressures, influences and circumstances that often discouraged his going to the field. One of the biggest was the sense of his own inadequacy. Only the fact that the Great Commission is framed on both sides with two tremendous statements on the part of the Lord Jesus Christ gave Abe courage to proceed: "All authority in heaven and earth has been given to Me . . . I am with you always" (Matthew 28:18, 20, *Living Gospels*).

These two promises clinched everything for him and brought the assurance that settled it all. After some twenty years of service in foreign lands, the Van Der Puys continue to stand on these promises.

Abe's very background, Holland Dutch, also seemed a hindrance to his going to the field. He came from a hard-working frugal people, a people who pride themselves in paying their bills and not being obligated to anyone, a people with fierce independence. With such a heart, the thought of being supported by or being dependent upon someone else was annoying to Abe. He admits, "It took a great deal of God's work in my heart to make me willing to accept support from others."

Abe's father had long hoped that when his son was grown he would become a Certified Public Accountant and enter the family business. The world of finance appealed to this young man and Abe says, "Even today when I read *Time* magazine, I turn first to the section on U.S. and world business."

He knew that any announcement of missionary intention would constitute a great disappointment to his father. Though it did at first, later all of the family gave him enthusiastic support. Abe could not escape the growing unshakable conviction that the Lord was separating him unto the Gospel. Here again it was a case of putting Jesus Christ first.

Abe summarizes God's dealings with him and his call to foreign service in these words:

"The effective ministry of worthy missionary representatives whose messages brought heart searching and a vision of a world without Christ was a great help to me. Consistent earnest prayer, both personally and in company with others, also helped me understand the will of God. I hold most firmly to the truth taught in Scripture, that when we seek we will find. God certainly led me a step at a time.

"I am thankful, too, for the encouragement of key Christian brethren who displayed keen interest in God's dealings with me and who were willing to add practical participation to their interest. The spontaneous help given by both individuals and churches seemed to confirm God's call to us. I would be amiss not to mention what it has meant to me to read outstanding biographies. I have done a lot of reading. Books like *The Triumph of John and Betty Stam* left an indelible impression upon my heart and life.

"One big factor, last but not least, was the spiritual communion and fellowship with a roommate. We did a good deal of praying together concerning God's will. It became increasingly clear that the Lord wanted me as a missionary and that Stan Harwood should serve as a Christian businessman. When this became evident to us, we prayed that God would make us a team and He has done just that. Stan has had a substantial part in our support for some twenty years.

"What a joy it is to be in missionary service. The night we first left for Quito our hearts were filled with joy to overflowing. We looked at each other and said, 'Thank God. This is it. We have pointed toward this time for several years and now it has come.' No two people could have been happier than we were when our plane took off."

CHAPTER 14

The "Dear John" Letter

My daughter Margaret Anne graduated from Culter Academy in Los Angeles that weekend. At the baccalaureate service I had eyes only for my sweet-sixteen.

The speaker was an angular man with a large forehead, gaunt cheeks, and a lopsided chin—not handsome but magnetic. Probably not yet thirty years old. His words soon captured my thoughts.

He spoke with power, with the authority of a man who knew the Scriptures, with the controlled energy of one whose experience of God was deep. As I listened to Ed Murphy that hot Sunday afternoon the conviction formed in my mind: *Murphy belongs in South America.*

I flipped over my program and reread the blurb on the Reverend Edward F. Murphy. Raised in the Catholic church. Biola graduate. Now a pastor in a Los Angeles suburb.

I resolved to speak to him after the service. The graduation throng and my daughter, so grownup in her crisp new suit, detained me in the church. But I caught Murphy outside crossing the street to his car.

"Man," I told him as we shook hands, "that was a great message, but I wish you had preached it

---

EDWARD F. MURPHY
Missionary to South America under
Overseas Crusades, Inc.
Overseas Crusades Associate Executive
Director for Ministries

---

in South America. I believe God wants you on the foreign mission field."

"Dr. Hillis," Ed replied, "I've been praying for months that God would show me exactly where He wants me. I am ready to go as soon as I know where and with what mission.

We made an appointment to talk about it that week. In my office Ed told me the amazing story of his missionary calling.

The name "Murphy" says Irish Catholic. Ed Murphy grew up in the Roman Catholic Church and was a devout, clean-living, loyal son of the church.

"Was it your conversion that made you leave Roman Catholicism?" I asked.

"No. Oddly enough, Dr. Hillis, my discovery that God wanted me to be a missionary forced me to break with my church. One of my friends raised the question, 'How are you going to be a missionary since you are a Roman Catholic? Will you enter the priesthood?'

"My answer startled *me*. 'No,' I replied instantly, 'I'm going to leave the Catholic church.'

"You see, Dr. Hillis, I realized that as a missionary I would have to preach salvation through Jesus Christ, not salvation through a church or its sacraments. Shall I tell you how I myself found salvation?"

I nodded and Mr. Murphy began his story.

In a summer forestry camp where he was working to save money for college, seventeen-year-old Ed looked for a friend whose conversation and conduct were clean. Soon he and Warren "Hutch" Hutchinson teamed up.

"Ed, are you a Christian?" Hutch asked as the two young men cleared a fire trail together one day.

"Why sure! I'm a Roman Catholic," replied Ed in surprise.

"I know that," said his friend, "but are you a Christian?"

Hutch went on to explain that a Christian has experienced personally the salvation Jesus came to provide.

Murphy cut him short. How could a Protestant,

separated from the true church, understand the things of God?

But deeply religious Murphy saw no reason why he should not have simple worship services with Protestant Hutch out among the California redwoods. Since there were no Sunday masses to attend, what harm could come from reading the Bible and praying together?

At first Murphy carried his missal to these quiet meetings. But more and more the words of the Scripture captivated him.

How simple and clear became the divine way of salvation as Ed heard and then read for himself the words of Jesus. The high school boy began to memorize: "I say emphatically that anyone who listens to My message and believes in God who sent me has eternal life, and will never be damned for his sins, but has already passed out of death into life" (John 5:24, *Living Gospels*).

Ed returned home in September a new creature in Christ but still an active Roman Catholic. His love for the New Testament which Hutch had given him was soon noticed by his family. They were upset by Ed's new religious concepts and arranged for him to attend indoctrination classes at the parish manse.

Yet the teaching of the priest could not take the place of the Word of God. Murphy read avidly. When forbidden to study the Scriptures at home he carried his New Testament to mass—it looked just like a missal—and read happily all through the service.

Graduating from high school, Ed followed his electrical interests and began training at a trade school in Chicago. He rented a tiny apartment and threw all his spare time into the study of the new Douay Bible that he had bought.

Murphy had always supposed that the average layman would have great difficulty reading the Bible. But he discovered that the Holy Spirit illumined the pages for him.

". . . Your own body does not belong to you, for God has bought you with a great price" (I Corinthians

6:19, 20, *Living Letters*) was the portion the divine light shone on one day.

For the first time Ed Murphy realized that by rights his life belonged to the Lord. The electrical career . . . was that God's plan for his life?

"O Lord," prayed the young student, "until now I did not know that I belonged only to you. Father, I am willing to do whatever you wish. Please show me your will."

Almost immediately, God showed him. Out of curiosity, Ed went to a Protestant church service with a friend. Neither the sermon nor the pastor impressed Murphy much. His friend left Ed waiting in the foyer for a few minutes after the service. A literature table stood nearby. Ed leafed through the magazines and pamphlets, picked up one, and took it home.

Carefully reading the booklet that night, Ed was stirred by the challenge of Christian missions. The pamphlet described the work of missionaries throughout the world. As Ed studied its message, the Holy Spirit engraved upon his heart the conviction that God wanted to use *him* in foreign service.

In the fall of 1948, Murphy knew he should leave school in Chicago and go home to California as his first step towards missionary service. But how was he to get the money for a two-thousand-mile trip? He could not ask his Catholic mother to loan him the money to quit electrical school, travel home, leave the Catholic church, and prepare himself for the mission field.

"A few days later," Ed states, "as I walked to school as usual, I was surprised to see a picket line around the school. Instructors and students were marching and carrying placards. The instructors had gone on strike for better working conditions.

"The school was closed down for some time. Every day I went to school hoping to attend classes, but I was always turned away by the pickets. 'Lord, what should I do now?' I prayed."

Obviously, by closing the door of the school God was opening Ed's door home. Now he could legitimately write and ask his mother to help him return to California. Soon Murphy was home again working to repay his mother's loan.

"Mom, God has called me to be a missionary," said Ed, coming right to the point as soon as he arrived home. "He has called me to preach the Gospel of His love and grace as taught in the Bible. I cannot reconcile this Gospel with many of the doctrines of our church, so I am leaving it. I want to prepare myself for the Lord's service."

Mrs. Murphy gaped at her son in amazement. She, of course, had known of Ed's love for the Bible and his "strange Protestant ideas." But she had never expected it to come to this.

"You are a Roman Catholic," she said, "and you will remain a Roman Catholic until you die. You are not going to leave your church. You are still my son and must do what I tell you."

Ed quietly replied that he must first obey God.

Through an aunt in Los Angeles he learned of Biola College. He was accepted as a student for the semester beginning in January. When Ed informed his mother, she was first furious, then heartbroken. In a few days she arranged an appointment for her son with the priest.

"My son," said the Reverend Father, when he and Ed were alone, "your life will end in ruin and the hand of God will be against you if you leave the church. The Roman Church is the only true church of Jesus Christ."

Murphy was only nineteen years old. All his knowledge of the Bible had come from his own private study during the past three years. How could he answer a learned priest? From the Catholic Bible, Ed showed the priest the basis for his faith in Christ and his decision to be a non-Catholic missionary.

"Father, no Protestant has led me astray. I am making my own decision on the basis of the Word of God."

"My son," returned the priest, "do you think you know the Scriptures better than we priests do? You are just a boy. You have not the training to enable you to interpret the Bible correctly. Only the Catholic church can expound its true teachings. You have read too much without guidance." And he offered Ed some books on Catholic doctrine.

Then the priest warned Ed of the consequences of a break with the church. Ed would disgrace his family with its Irish Catholic tradition. He would be deserting his widowed mother in her hour of need. And he would bring down the judgments of God upon his head by forsaking the only storehouse of God's grace through which a man's soul could be saved.

Finally, seeing that Murphy turned to the Scriptures to counter each argument, the priest said, "The Bible commands children to obey their parents. Your mother has forbidden you to leave the Catholic church. If you disobey her, you will be disobeying the Bible which you claim is your guide for life."

What could the young Christian say to that? "Well, Father, I never thought of it that way before. The Bible certainly says, 'Children, obey your parents' (Ephesians 6:1). Therefore until my mother consents or until I am twenty-one, I suppose I cannot leave the Catholic church or begin my missionary training."

The priest went home in triumph and Mrs. Murphy heard the news with great delight. But Ed was in turmoil. For weeks his heart was torn in two directions.

"At last, Dr. Hillis, a ray of light seemed to shine on Jesus' words: 'I have come to set a man against his father, and . . . mother . . . But if you love your father and mother more than you love Me, you are not worthy of being Mine' (Matthew 10:35, 37, *Living Gospels*).

"I saw that my mother had placed herself in the way of God in my life. I realized that I must obey God even if in doing so I had to disobey my mother.

" 'Mom,' I told her, 'I clearly see the will of God for my life. He has called me to preach the Gospel of His grace which comes to men through Jesus Christ, not through any one church, its priesthood or sacraments. I know you do not understand, but I must obey Christ and His Word.'

"For several hours we talked. Mother argued and pleaded. What agony for us both! Finally, weeping hysterically, Mother ran from the room crying, 'If you leave the church you are no son of mine.'

"Heartbroken, I packed my bags. I left my church, my home, and my embittered mother, and entered Biola College."

"Studies were hard at Biola," Murphy resumed his story. "I entered school at mid-year, and I hadn't the evangelical background of my fellow students. Often the phraseology and terminology used by the professors completely lost me. However, teachers and students helped me kindly. For a hungry new Christian, it was a thrilling experience.

"Then one morning I awoke to the thought, *What if the Roman Catholic Church is the only church of Jesus Christ after all? If the Roman church is true, then Ed Murphy is doomed to hell.*

"I was conscious of an evil presence in the room with me. Perhaps this sounds melodramatic to you, Dr. Hillis, but I felt that the Devil was standing there to claim me. What terrible oppression! I could not get out of bed. I was physically sick, mentally and emotionally tormented.

"I didn't go to classes that morning. I spent the whole day in bed, saying I was ill. How could I explain what was going on inside me?

"I knew that Jesus said, 'But some will come to Me—those the Father has given Me—and I will never, never reject them' (John 6:37, *Living Gospels*). I knew Jesus said, 'I give them eternal life, and they shall never perish. No one shall snatch them away from Me' (John 10:28, *Living Gospels*).

"Yet my heart was filled with terror and torment. I could not escape that accusing question, *What if the Roman church is right? Then you are doomed to hell.*

"Eventually I told my roommate what was happening to me. Soon many of the students were praying for me. Still I could not leave my bed or free myself of the awful fear that seemed to possess me.

"The third day was an all-school day of prayer, culminating in a united prayer meeting after supper. With my roommate's help, I got up and went to the auditorium. I sat down and tried to pray in my heart with the other students. At last, though I had never before prayed in public, I stood to my feet and cried out to God to deliver me from this terrible oppression. Immediately the evil presence with its fearsome accusations left me, and the joy of the Lord flooded my soul."

"Never again," continued Murphy, relief and gratitude shining in his grey eyes, "have I suffered such a demonic attack or been tempted to doubt the saving grace of God. 'No weapon that is formed against thee shall prosper,' says Isaiah 54:17. But all this time another weapon was being formed against me, and this last one came closer than any of the others to breaking my will to serve God."

"You survived your mother's grief, the priest's arguments, and demonic oppression," I interposed. "I am surprised anything else could shake you, Ed."

"My fiancee wrote saying she would break our engagement if I persisted in my plans to become a missionary." Murphy's large eyes clouded at the memory.

"I told you, Dr. Hillis, that I had a pretty sweetheart. We had fallen in love when she was just a freshman in high school. We planned to marry in the summer after my first term at Biola. Lovely Loretta, sweet and sensitive! I dreamed of serving the Lord with her at my side. I knew she would follow me anywhere. When we first went together, she had agreed to join the Catholic church to marry me. And now that she was a born-again Christian I looked forward blissfully to our marriage and missionary work together."

"Then all of a sudden a 'Dear John' letter. Why?"

"Mother felt that the surest way to force me to abandon my plans for the Christian ministry would be through my love for Loretta. Loretta was young, impressionable, new in the faith. If she could be persuaded that she was not suited to mission work, perhaps she could talk me out of my commitment."

As a counselor of missionary candidates, I could well imagine the tack Mrs. Murphy had taken with Loretta.

"Loretta, do you really think that you have been made for that type of life? A delicate girl like you? Do you realize that missionaries live in grass huts in the jungle? You would have to carry water from a muddy river and boil it before you could drink it. Are you physically strong enough to keep house under such conditions?

"We really don't believe you have thought what such a move would involve. There's no sanitation and little medical care in those far-away lands. Your children would be born without a doctor's help. Sickness and dirt and evil climate would threaten their innocent lives. You'd better work on Ed now to get him to change his mind if you want a happy life and a healthy family.

"Tell Ed you are not the girl for missionary life. He'll change his plans for your sake. He might even come home from Bible school and go back to his electrical work. Then you could get married right away. He has three years of study ahead unless you can get him to see how unreasonable his missionary dream is."

Poor Loretta. A few months of that kind of pressure and no wonder she wrote Ed to cancel his plans, either for the mission field or for marriage.

"What did you do, Ed?" I asked.

"I left Biola right away, without even asking permission from the dean of men. I could have been expelled for that, Dr. Hillis, but I did not care. All that mattered was my poor scared sweetheart.

"I stayed home a week, trying to comfort and encourage her. But Loretta refused to consider being a missionary's wife. Eventually it came to a showdown. Loretta said I must choose between marrying her and being a missionary. I was heartbroken. I begged the Lord to change her mind. He seemed to say to me just what she had said, 'Which do you love best, Loretta or my will for you?'

"Dr. Hillis, I actually made plans to quit Biola. But God gave me strength to obey Him and faith to trust my life to His care.

"I went back to school, no longer engaged to the girl I deeply loved. I confess I had to continually fight the temptation to give up and go back to her.

"Before the school year was out, Loretta wrote that God had spoken to her. She confessed that she loved me and would serve God with me anywhere in the world.

"My mother was terribly upset. All her efforts had failed. Without telling me, she began to search the Scriptures and pray that God would help her to find His truth. When I arrived home for vacation after my second year at Biola, Mother greeted me with a radiant face.

" 'Ed,' she said, hugging me, 'Jesus Christ is my personal Savior and Lord. I have placed all my confidence in His saving death and resurrection.' "

Ed paused, a wide smile wreathing his face as he remembered that happy meeting.

"Great, man. Marvelous," I exclaimed, as soon as I could trust my voice. "Everybody reconciled at last . . . you, your mother, Loretta. That is just the way God does things.

"But, Ed, you have been out of school six years. Why aren't you on the mission field?"

"I guess maybe I've been waiting to meet you, Dr. Hillis," said Murphy, grinning disarmingly. "Loretta and I applied to go to India right after graduation, but the Indian government turned down our visas. So we took a pastorate here in California.

"But lately I have been getting restless. I've corresponded with several missions. Right now I have application forms on my office desk all ready to mail. I have been asking the Lord, 'Where shall I go and with what mission?' And I've had a growing conviction that somehow, when the right time arrived, God would let me know.

"As I spoke to the Culter graduating class last Sunday, I spotted you in the audience, Dr. Hillis. I recognized you from hearing you in missionary conferences and from the Overseas Crusades literature I have been reading for years. Right away I thought, *Perhaps God will use Dr. Hillis to show me where and with what mission I should serve.*

"When you hailed me outside the church and said, 'Ed, God wants you on the mission field,' my heart said, *This is it.* So here I am, boss. Do you have a job for me?"

"God has a job for you," I replied, "in South America."

CHAPTER 15

Unqualified

Lilian choked down the lump in her throat, but she knew she could not hide the tears in her eyes. Her hopes had been smashed again, and this time she had been so sure.

Once more she pleaded with the kind-looking women at the table, "But I've been training for years to go to China as a missionary. I *know* it is God's will for my life. I know it is!"

The members of the China Inland Mission Women's Council looked sadly at Lilian and shook their heads. "We are sorry," said the chairman. "We wish we could accept you, but we dare not send any new missionaries out during this war. It is not safe —especially for a woman. God must have another plan for you."

Minutes later Lilian knelt beside her bed and tried to pray. But all she could do was remember the years -almost ten of them—since she had known God wanted her in China. Why had she been disappointed so many times? Why?

As her sobbing quieted, Lilian seemed to hear God asking her, "Which is your first love, Lilian, China or Me?"

Immediately the curly-haired girl understood the lesson God had for her. "Forgive me," she prayed.

LILIAN HAMER
Missionary to China and Thailand
under the China Inland Mission
Nurse and Martyr

"I have not always put You first, but I give myself again completely to You. I will pay any price—even my life—to serve You as You wish."

As Lilian got up from her knees there was a new peace and determination in her heart. Little did she realize, as she dried her eyes, that some day she would pay the ultimate price—her life—to serve God.

Lilian Hamer was really not a very out-of-the-ordinary girl. If you had seen her in a crowd, you might have noted the mop of curly hair and the twinkle in her eye, but you would not have guessed the courage and determination that were so much a part of her character.

Her background was pretty ordinary, too—at least until she was nineteen. Born in 1910 and raised in the Lancashire district of England, Lilian did what the majority of the young girls in her home town did—she finished school at fourteen and went to work in the textile mills. It is hard for us to imagine a fun-loving teen-ager working ten hours a day, six days a week in a factory. But when all your friends are doing it, you can get used to it. Lilian must have enjoyed her job, for in less than five years she had worked her way up to a weaver's position.

Lilian was, of course, a "Christian"—and all her friends were "Christians"—for wasn't England a Christian nation? She went to church, well, almost every Sunday. Then one Sunday she attended a Methodist Church and for the first time in her life heard the message of Christ's salvation. When the invitation was given, Lilian walked down the aisle to become a real Christian.

The routine of Lilian's life was now interrupted. She had something to live and work for. She did not know what God wanted her to do in life, so she began to develop every gift she had. She went to night school and studied elocution, dressmaking and first aid. Then one night, at a China Inland Mission meeting, Lilian felt God was calling her to missionary work in China. Life now had a new direction.

Lilian felt that God could best use her as a nurse on the mission field, so she began nurses' training at Bolton District Hospital. Here her gay spirits were a delight to her fellow workers and her patients. She had a merry sense of humor that could cheer up the gloomiest patient. Near the end of her training she applied to the C.I.M. To her great surprise and disappointment she was rejected.

After studying midwifery for a year, she applied again and was rejected. It was 1941 and the war was on. This second "No" stunned Lilian. Had she mistaken God's voice? When she prayed, her convictions about China became stronger. She swallowed her disappointment and enrolled in the two-year course at Radcliffe Missionary Training College. After graduation, she applied for the third time and received the heartbreaking answer from the Women's Council as previously related.

Lilian Hamer, I said, was really not a very out-of-the-ordinary girl. I underrated her. Where is the girl today who, turned down three times for foreign service, will still not give up? With bulldog tenacity she held on. Like a flint, her face was set toward China and somehow she would get there.

She heard that the Red Cross was looking for nurses to care for the Chinese wounded, and she jumped at the chance to reach the land she loved. After a semester of studying the Chinese language, Lilian boarded the ship that would carry her to China.

It may have been bleak, cold weather that February day in 1944, but Lilian's heart was full of joy. This wasn't the way she would have planned things. She had pictured herself leaving England with a band of other missionaries—not Red Cross doctors and nurses. But God's ways were higher than her ways, and she was happy.

The scenes which greeted Lilian in Southwest China were not very pleasant. Beside the roadside and in filthy huts she cared for the wounded Chinese soldiers. The Japanese were gaining ground rapidly, pushing the Chinese back until the little Red Cross band was forced to evacuate, losing all their supplies.

After just a few weeks in China, Lilian was faced with the possibility of being sent back to England.

She sent another application to the China Inland Mission, praying more earnestly than ever before. Perhaps the fact that she was in China now and that she could speak a little of the language would make a difference. It did. After more than ten years of training, waiting, and praying, Lilian Hamer became a full-fledged missionary!

Her first appointment was to a pioneer hospital in the mountainous Tali area. There she was in charge of the maternity wards. How she loved her work! Every day she brought black-eyed noisy babies into the world and every day she talked to their mothers about Jesus. Her quick sense of humor once again endeared her to staff and patients alike—not that she was perfect. Occasionally her temper was as quick as her sense of humor!

One day (probably a busy fourteen-hour day as usual) Lilian noticed some unfamiliar women in the waiting room. They did not dress like the Chinese and their dialect was strange. She learned that they were from a mountain tribe known as the Miao. They told her of the thousands of tribespeople in the high mountains to the south and west. There were no missionaries among these people . . . no nurses.

As Lilian went about her daily duties at the hospital, more and more her heart was occupied with the tribespeople. When she stood at her window at dusk and watched the sun setting on the mountain ranges, she prayed fervently that God would send her to tell the tribespeople before it was too late.

It was now 1948 and there was trouble at the hospital. The Communists were slowly conquering China and spreading resentment toward the missionaries. Eventually, even the hospital grounds were taken over, and Lilian and her co-workers were forced to flee. At once Lilian's thoughts flew to the mountains. She asked the mission to send her to the Lisu in Thailand.

There was hesitation on the part of the mission leaders. Was it safe to allow a single woman to live in the hills? They thought not. But when Tao Lu, a Christian headman of the Yao Tribe, pleaded for medical help, Lilian was sent into the mountains.

This was the first of Lilian's many mountain treks, but no woman could ever become used to the hours of arduous hiking. Lilian never complained during these all-day treks. She could even joke about her bleeding feet or the times when she would slip off the narrow trail and fall into the flooded rice paddies or the fact that she was always the farthest behind in any group of hikers.

The Yao built Lilian a tiny shack with split bamboo walls and a mud floor. In it there was room for only a cot and a crate that was used as a table. From sunup until sundown Lilian treated patients on her small porch. The majority of these patients were opium smokers who wanted to break the habit. They knew opium was ruining their lives—it made them weak and sick so they could not work their tiny farms—and they heard Lilian had medicine to cure them.

For two years Lilian lived among the Yao, teaching their children, delivering their babies, and healing their sick. It was discouraging work, for very few of them became Christians. It would be several years later before the harvest would be reaped among the Yao.

Higher up in the mountains lived the Lisu. Sometimes they came down to Lilian's small clinic for treatment and before they left Lilian would always promise, "If you will build me a hut, I will come to your village."

Every day she prayed that soon the Lisu would really want her. And then one day she received word that a hut had been built for her and she was to come as soon as possible. How great was her anticipation as she began the two-and-a-half-hour hike to the Lisu village and how great was her disappointment when she saw her new "home"—a tiny shack even smaller than the one at the Yao village.

"We thought that this little shack would be big enough for you, as you are only one," explained the headman. Lilian rarely complained, but the conditions took a toll of her health. She ate and slept on the floor and usually had a backache because her roof was not high enough to allow her to stand erect.

During the day she treated scores of patients and taught the people about the true God who was more powerful than demons.

Gradually the Lisu began to respond to the message of Christ. The village headman, Khun Ba, became a Christian and refused to worship demons any longer. The people waited fearfully for him to die in some sudden manner, but when nothing happened others began to take courage and leave demon worship. Lilian was jubilant. The months of physical weariness and spiritual loneliness had been worth it!

The Lisu had finally promised to build her a larger house, so Lilian went back to the Yao village to get her furniture and spend a few days with her friends there. Imagine her dismay when she found, upon returning to the Lisu village, that her house was not finished. In fact, tribesmen were actually tearing down what they had just built. It seems that her new house had been started on "Demon Hill" and the people had become too frightened to work there any longer.

Lilian wrote home, "As I write, I can hear men pulling down the house. It would seem as if the spirits on the hill are laughing triumphantly. But the missionary at the foot of Demon Hill stands at the door of her shack and laughs too, for a great victory shall be the end result of this seeming failure."

And the victory was great—not in terms of numbers. But God does not count numbers as we do.

Lilian always wanted to go higher. She could never forget the tribes "beyond." She began to make trips to other villages, giving medical help and telling about Jesus Christ. In 1958 Lilian moved into a shack in the village of Banlaung. Although she never complained, her letters revealed some of the constant physical weariness she endured.

During the day she treated scores of patients. At night the wild demon dances kept her awake. Loneliness had never become easier to bear. Lilian had been alone now for ten years, except for a brief furlough and occasional visits from fellow missionaries. She was just as human as you or I, so we know she became discouraged. But she was a faithful soldier of Jesus Christ and was never defeated!

One Saturday in April, Lilian decided to go down to the valley, an all-day hike. It would be good for her to have a quiet peaceful Sunday. Besides, she was almost out of medical supplies. She started the long trek through the jungles. We will never know what her thoughts were that morning. But we do know that she often sang hymns as she walked. Perhaps she was doing just that when suddenly a man stepped from between two large trees and shot Lilian with a sawed-off shotgun. She died instantly.

The murderer was never captured. Who was he? What did he want? We will never know. But Lilian Hamer's life is more important to us than how she died. Was it worth it all—the years of training and disappointments followed by only a handful of converts and a violent death?

If we could talk to Lilian she would have but one answer. She would remind us of the one picture in her tiny hut, a picture of Christ walking into the future, looking back over His shoulder to see who was following Him. Lilian Hamer was—and He was worth it all.

Few stories have been harder to write than this one. While writing, my mind has traveled those lonely tribal trails. I saw the devil fetishes, sensed the hot breath of Satan, and shuddered at the heat of the spiritual battle. Warfare, I thought to myself, is not for girls but for men. I am a man. Did Lilian Hamer, a girl, have more determination to know and do the will of God than I, a man? Is God using women in front line warfare because He cannot find men?

CHAPTER 16

"You Are a Fool"

The great three-headed Kali, goddess of war and vengeance, glared down upon her worshippers. Four American college boys stared back at the many-armed idol in awe. For the first time they were viewing raw paganism.

The thin Brahma, the orange-robed priests, the hideous idols made an indelible impression upon Bill Gillam, first tenor of the quartet. There was a stench about the place—a stench from the great pool of holy water, where the Hindus bathed and drank; a stench from the altar rack where animals were sacrificed to Kali, their blood thrown upon the face of the fearsome deity to appease her thirst and to atone for the sins of the worshippers.

Inside Gillam rose a fierce desire to shout from the pinnacles of the immense temple, "The blood of Jesus Christ, God's Son, cleanses from all sin."

Standing by the iron gates with his three companions, Bill Gillam received his missionary call—simply the knowledge that God wanted him to help reach the heathen world with the Gospel of redeeming love.

When Gillam agreed to join the year-long missionary tour of the college quartet he suspected that something like this might happen. His mother had raised Bill with the prayer that he would give his life to the Christian ministry.

DR. WILLIAM A. GILLAM
Missionary to Colombia under
The Oriental Missionary Society
Vice President of The Oriental Missionary Society

When Bill finished high school in 1932, he and his mother began working to save money for a Christian college education. But America was struggling to drag itself out of the depression and, after three years, Bill had only $100.

He would have to take his education on faith. Bill learned that at Asbury College, a Christian school, he could work for his room. So he packed his bags, folded his initial funds into his wallet, and hitchhiked to Wilmore, Kentucky.

At Asbury, musical Gillam lost no time in striking up barbershop harmony with three other freshmen. Like other Gospel quartets on campus, they sang in nearby churches and in evangelistic campaigns.

One May evening a knock roused Bill from his studies. The dorm monitor Mac wanted to talk to him. Perching himself on a corner of the desk, Mac told Gillam that evangelist Dr. John Thomas had invited the Asbury Ambassadors, the best quartet on campus, to join him in a world missionary tour.

Mac explained the itinerary for the year. "And, Bill," he concluded, swinging a leg casually against the desk, "we'd like you to come along as first tenor."

"Me?" asked Gillam, startled. "Can't Johnny Smith make the trip?"

"No," said Mac, "Johnny asked his girl if they could postpone their wedding for a year while he traveled with us. But they have been going together a long time. Janie told Johnny he'd marry her now or never."

So Johnny married Janie and Bill Gillam went around the world as first tenor of the Asbury Ambassadors.

Gillam had a girl to think of, too. As the tour got under way, Bill wrote Mary enthusiastic reports of the campaigns in the British Isles. But soon a sobering thought disturbed him. What if God wanted him in overseas service? Would Mary want to pursue their friendship if cobras and contaminated water were in prospect? Or would she, like Janie, say, "Me or missions"?

Picture Gillam in a church house in London. His blond head bends over a pad of air-weight paper. The pen squeaks out a few slow words. Then Bill sits back and gazes thoughtfully out the window, hardly seeing the trolleys, the cars, the charcoal vendor in his horsecart. Back over the paper again and a few more words.

A ticklish task. It took Bill about fourteen pages to express himself to his satisfaction. Without actually committing himself to a proposal of marriage, Bill wanted to ask Mary if she would consider being a missionary's wife in case God should call him into service abroad.

You know the kind of letter. You know how badly Bill's pen tip was chewed before he signed the last page and how many times, as he waited for an answer, Bill thought of ways he could have worded it better.

In South Africa several weeks later Bill eagerly opened Mary's reply. As she prayed over his letter, Mary wrote, the Spirit of God asked her another question. Not would she be willing to go to the mission field with Bill as her husband but would she be willing to serve God in some foreign land *alone*? Yes, came Mary's thoughtful answer. Married or single, she wanted to follow God's leading. She wanted only God's will.

Rejoicing that Mary responded so readily to the idea of missionary service, Bill Gillam kept his eyes and ears open during the year's travels. South Africa, India, Hong Kong, China, Korea, Japan—the quartet blended their voices in American Gospel songs and learned simple choruses in the native languages of the countries they visited. Dr. Thomas gave stirring messages, translated by local evangelists. Missionaries rejoiced in the breath of home that the team brought.

One June morning in beautiful Peking, Dr. Thomas spoke at The Oriental Missionary Society Bible school. At the close of the sermon a blue-gowned student walked to the front of the chapel, laid a quilt across the altar, and addressed the congregation earnestly in Chinese.

What was that all about? Gillam wondered. After the service he asked a missionary.

"The *p'u-qai*, or wadded quilt, serves as both mattress and blanket here in North China," explained

Dr. Erny. "The student who gave his testimony owns very little except his warm *p'u-qai*. He put the quilt on the altar as a sign that he gives himself and all he possesses to the Lord."

The young student's act of consecration profoundly impressed Bill Gillam. Am I willing to do as much for the Gospel? he asked himself.

Another incident, seemingly trivial, clinched for Bill his missionary calling. In Korea, missionaries treated the team to a delightful supper party around a brightly decorated table. Above each fork perched a place card with not a name but a career.

Bill looked for an appropriate place for himself. No, not college professor; that would be Mac. Not evangelistic singer; that would be Joe. Professional writer—heaven forbid! The only place that seemed to fit was labeled "Future Missionary."

As Bill hitched his chair up to the table, the little card before him seemed bigger than a billboard. God was advertising . . . "Places for future missionaries" . . . and Bill Gillam filled one place.

Gillam had seen the need of the heathen. He cleared the decks for action by facing and dealing with his personal obligations. He took to heart examples of consecrated living. He watched for and recognized the finger of God pointing to him.

He would be a missionary. But where?

Bill finished his college work at Asbury, married loyal Mary, and entered seminary. Graduation loomed ahead and Bill wondered, "Where should I go?"

He filled out an application form for The Oriental Missionary Society. "To what field do you feel called?" The question stared him in the face.

Every land the quartet had visited on tour had stimulated in Gillam a sense of responsibility for the heathen. Perhaps the needs of India weighed heaviest on his heart. But Bill felt no definite "call" to India, China, Africa. He knew, simply, that God wanted him to reach the lost abroad.

Bill dipped his pen and wrote, "I do not have any specific field call, but God has especially burdened my heart for India."

Today Gillam, as a mission executive, says, "Young people uncertain about their placement should be encouraged to move forward on the best light and the deepest burden they have."

Bill and Mary Gillam moved forward and faced, suddenly, a slammed door. They were all ready to cross the Pacific when Pearl Harbor exploded their plans.

Evangelistic meetings, an Indiana pastorate—the Gillams marked time while America was at war.

God had two things for Bill in that delay—pastoral experience, a vital prerequisite for general missionary service, and redirection. One after another, during those two years, Gillam met the men and women who were spearheading The Oriental Missionary Society's advance into Latin America. By August, 1943, the Gillams knew God wanted them in South America.

Vocation—missionary. Location—Colombia. God had shown Bill the way step by step.

The Gillams worked in South America until 1956. Bill composed hymns in Spanish for the growing evangelical churches of Colombia. He assisted in the outreach of South American Youth for Christ evangelism.

As Field Director of The Oriental Missionary Society work in Colombia, Ecuador, and Brazil, Mr. Gillam traveled extensively on evangelistic campaigns and supervisory missions.

In 1956, The O.M.S. Board of Directors asked Gillam to assume responsibilities temporarily in the homeland. Again Bill's sense that he was called to reach the lost, not called to a particular place, gave him grace to leave the land he had learned to love and accept the mission assignment as Director of Home Ministries.

Suavely handsome, briefcase in hand, Mr. Gillam today looks like any other Indianapolis executive. But ask him to sing a Spanish Gospel song. His face lights up. His blue eyes shine behind his sober glasses. He reaches for his accordion.

"You know, Dick," he says, dropping the accordion when the last full chord has died away, "I would love to be back in Colombia now. But when I first went there in 1943 it was like breaking the sound barrier. Opposition all the way."

"I will never forget our last night in the States," continues Bill, leaning forward in his swivel chair. "We waited in a New Orleans hotel room for a midnight flight to Panama. Judy, our toddler, napped on the bed. Mary gave Linda a bottle and rocked her to sleep in the armchair.

"I sat on the window sill and looked out over the city in the quiet of the night, the lights sparkling below me. The Devil came and sat down beside me. I know what his voice is like, Dick. I've heard his subtle insinuations many times.

"*'Bill, you are a fool,'* he told me. *'Why don't you go back to Indiana? What are you doing taking your wife and children off to a strange land? There's no work in Colombia for you, no Protestant church. You don't know anybody in the whole country. Why don't you go back home?'*

"Only God's grace brought me through that hour of temptation," Mr. Gillam confesses.

In spite of all of Satan's arguments, midnight found the Gillams winging out over the Gulf of Mexico. The next day another plane took them from Panama over the beautiful Andes Ranges to Medellin.

A distinguished looking gentleman sat across the aisle from the young family. He glanced curiously at Bill several times during the flight and finally asked, "Young man, what may your business be?"

"I am a missionary," Bill answered.

The elderly gentleman smiled sadly and condescendingly. "Do you mean you are a Protestant missionary?"

"Yes."

"Now, young man, I have traveled considerably in Latin America. All of the people in Colombia where you are going are already Christians. They are fine Catholics. What makes you think you are needed?"

It seemed to Gillam as though the Devil was taunting him again. "*You see what I told you, Bill? Why don't you go back home instead of trying this thing?*"

The plane circled down over Medellin, beautiful capital of Colombia. "I looked down at the city," remembers Mr. Gillam. "I saw the twin spires of the Metropolitan Cathedral, and I realized that the Devil had told me the truth. I was entering one of the great citadels of the Roman Catholic religion. What could I, a young missionary, do to bring the light of the free grace of God into that bastion of Catholicism?"

Though the spiritual skirmishes were real enough to the new missionary, some of the opposition Bill faced took more concrete form.

One Sunday morning, during Bill's first year in Colombia, he accompanied a small missionary team out into the eastern mountain range for a morning service in the village of La Union. The owner of the house had forgotten his key, so "church" was held on the sidewalk near the parked car.

Gillam played his accordion and sang what songs he knew in Spanish. A crowd gathered quickly, villagers in Sunday best, most of them on their way to or from Mass. They listened in a stalwart silence that combined curiosity and hostility.

As the preacher finished his sermon, rocks began to rain down on the missionaries' car. Shouts went up, "Viva la Virgin. Long live the Virgin. Down with the Protestants." The villagers massed to attack.

Gillam and his friends jumped into the car and made their escape through the angry mob, which divided down the middle like the Red Sea to let God's people through.

"Missionaries must face such experiences in today's world of crisis and chaos," believes Mr. Gillam. "Satanic power seeks to destroy our witness. Only the indwelling fullness of the Holy Spirit in all His power can bring victory."

Who called Bill Gillam a fool?

CHAPTER 17

Tea Bags and Rope Holders

Thompson must have chuckled over my despairing epistles. As newly appointed acting superintendent of the China Inland Mission work in war-devastated Honan, I needed help. The main problem—mission stations "manned" only by women.

How could we build a sturdy national church when there were so few missionaries to work with the men? And what about the strong-minded *Hsiao-jieh* (spinster) who refused to turn over the control of the local church to the Chinese pastor?

In letter after letter I poured out my difficulties to R. E. Thompson, Director of the C.I.M. work in North China. Every response from R.E. revealed loving sympathy, good humor, and a victorious assurance that God was bigger than my problems.

Thompson's Irish optimism and the unquenchable twinkle in his eye—how had these survived thirty years in the harsh Orient? And what made me instinctively trust his encouragement and counsel?

Thompson was a man groomed by God for the demanding task of helping other missionaries. Was the worker frustrated by government red tape? Thompson understood. For two years he had worked in Peking as the C.I.M. liaison man. His chief task, wading through the mounds of governmental minutia which the Japanese military regime required of the mission.

R. E. THOMPSON
Missionary to China
Regional Director of China Inland Mission
Founder of Missionary Internship

Was a young mother brooding over a child gone half a continent away to boarding school? Thompson's wife and children were captured by the Japanese and held by them in a concentration camp for four long silent years. R.E. understood loneliness.

Did the Chinese language sound like a tape recorder running backwards? Thompson sympathized. He had served in two parts of China where local dialects were so different from what he had learned in language school that he had to start all over again.

Had personal tragedy felled the missionary? The Thompsons had lost two of their five children. Three-year-old Evelyn died of diphtheria in the province of Hopeh, ten hours' rail journey from a doctor. And Brian, the eldest son, was electrocuted in a tragic accident during the Japanese internment.

Like Paul, Thompson could say to his junior missionaries, "What a wonderful God we have—He is the Father of our Lord Jesus Christ, the source of every mercy, and the One Who so wonderfully comforts and strengthens us in our hardships and trials. And why does He do this? That when others are troubled, needing our sympathy and encouragement, we can pass on to them this same help and comfort God has given us" (II Corinthians 1:3, 4, *Living Letters*).

Thompson emerged from the trials of war and bereavement white-haired but with a God-given buoyancy of spirit. As a regional director of the China Inland Mission, R.E. traveled through eleven vast provinces, sharing joy and comfort with the scattered missionaries.

Smiling nostalgically, he conjures up word pictures of those trips: "I journeyed hundreds of miles by truck up and down the Burma Road, sitting on top of the truck loads with ten or twelve Chinese. The untrained Chinese drivers careened recklessly down the mountain sides and swung around the narrow corners.

"At the end of the long uncomfortable ride was a little city where half a dozen or perhaps twenty missionaries waited for fellowship and the ministry of the Word. I would spend a week with them. In the living room of the mission home we would all study the Scriptures together, share a simple communion, and kneel to pray.

"Then quietly I would meet with them singly, in the guest room or the office. Over steaming bowls of Chinese tea they would confess their problems and difficulties. Prayerfully, I gave them counsel, comfort, and direction in their work."

"I came to a fuller and deeper realization of my fellow missionaries' many spiritual, mental, and physical needs," says R.E. in retrospect. "God was at work preparing my heart and mind for the work of Missionary Internship."

Missionary Internship, founded by Mr. Thompson in Detroit in 1953, is a training program for missionary candidates. Fifty mission boards send their young appointees there for supervised practical work in local churches and for counseling by the professional staff. So many pitfalls, so many missionary casualties, can be avoided by this kind of orientation.

R. E. Thompson's own missionary orientation had been informal but effective. By the time he first sailed for China in 1920, Thompson's life was demonstrating three traits essential to successful missionary service: initiative . . . obedience . . . and a vital relationship to Christ.

Missions look for men who are self-directed, self-disciplined achievers. Often the missionary must be placed on a lonely station without supervision or detailed instruction from mission headquarters. Will he grasp the potentialities of his location and muster his best energies to meet the challenge? Or will he gather wool?

From childhood Ernest Thompson was a go-getter. His parents often invited missionary speakers home from church for a meal or a night's lodging. Their exotic adventures fascinated little Ernest. He decided to work harder to fill his missionary bank.

What could a ten-year-old do? He chopped firewood and vended bundles of kindling from door to door. But that was not enough. Missions is big business, and the Thompson boy wanted to make a larger investment.

One day the pastor of Great Victoria Street Baptist Church announced to his congregation that Ernest Thompson was selling tea, all profits to go to missions, and that he would call on them. With a ten-shilling loan from his father, the ingenious towhead had gone into the tea business. He bought tea wholesale from a helpful Christian merchant and retailed it around the parish. For several years, Friday and Saturday afternoons and evenings were "tea time" for Thompson, as he trudged the streets of Belfast with his shoulder sack full of little packets of Ceylon tea.

Ernest's involvement with missions was infectious. A group of young people gathered around him for missionary focus every Thursday evening. One Thursday would see them in the Thompson living room, heads bent together over an atlas of China, learning the names of cities, rivers, and provinces. The next week they would cluster around a table to make splints and roll bandages, with all the merriment that a bunch of thirteen- and fourteen-year-olds can bring to the most clinical task.

When a missionary from the China Inland Mission spoke at Great Victoria Street Baptist Church, Ernest invited him home to meet the Rope Holders.

"Rope Holders!" echoed the missionary in astonishment.

"That's the name of our missionary league," explained the Thompson boy. "When William Carey was going to India he said he would go down the mine (India) for buried treasure if those at home would hold the ropes."

The visitor was delighted by the dedication of the young Rope Holders. He showed them pictures of China and they prayed for his work. The missionary left deeply enriched.

But the blessing was not one-sided. Ernest Thompson, too, was touched. He had been awed to see a grown man weep for the need of China. In his own room after the meeting, the boy made a contract with God for service in the land of China.

Now Thompson knew where he was going, and he was the kind of fellow who would get there. Still, many dedicated go-getters fail on the mission field. Why?

They cannot survive the trials and testings. The bad breath of decaying immorality and the fierce wind of Satanic opposition dry up their shallow spiritual experience. They know all the right doctrines, but their emotions do not correspond to the Scriptural promises. Soon questions are raised, and they are driven to doubt or despair.

Thompson, like many children raised in Christian homes, faced this crisis in his teens. He still remembers it vividly.

"Having been led to the Lord as a little boy, the depth of my experience was not very great. In my early teens I began to discover how shallow my Christian life really was. My thought life was the area in which Satan made his most vicious attacks. I felt unclean. I began to lose interest in Bible reading and prayer. But I am glad to say I continued to attend the young people's meetings, Sunday school, and church.

"My advice to young people going through such a period is to continue to go through the motions of Christianity regardless of how they may feel. God allows us to hunger so that we will be truly eager for the next step He has for us. He wants us to realize our own shallowness and spiritual inadequacy. And He wants to teach us the discipline of obedience even when the rewards of blessing are temporarily withdrawn.

"Satan will tempt you to doubt that your original decision for Christ was real at all. But hold on, and God will prove that He always has more of Himself ahead for you."

Thompson held on, in a guilty and frustrated sort of way. He learned of a fellowship meeting that was held every Friday night. Hungry, he attended. The meeting was left open for testimony. The Spirit of God urged him to give his testimony.

"Me, testify?" objected young Ernest. *"What do I have to say to these people? They are miles ahead of me spiritually. It would be presumptuous. It would be dishonest."*

But he could not silence the voice of the Lord, which kept urging him to give witness to God's grace in his life. At last he dragged himself to his feet and said lamely, "I'm glad Jesus is my Savior. My sins are forgiven. And I believe God has called me to be a missionary in China."

He sat down. It was like stepping into an elevator and going up ten floors! Thompson's obedience, reluctant as it was, had pushed open a door through which God poured the stunning reality of Himself in His Third Person. Henceforth the inner presence of the Holy Spirit would make Christ real to Thompson.

"That Friday night transformed me," testifies R.E. today. "The Word of God came to life. I discovered the excitement of prayer and the thrill of Christian fellowship. On the following Sunday night while attending a Gospel service I had the privilege of pointing a young person to my Savior. I was beginning to be a missionary."

"At the age of seventeen," Ernest continues, "I was under such a deep sense of the call of God to full-time service, I applied to a home mission known as The Faith Mission, working in Scotland and Northern Ireland. When I was eighteen I was accepted for training in the mission's school in Edinburgh, Scotland.

"I was very young and inexperienced in the things of God, and this was no ordinary school. Time each day was set aside for individual waiting on God. All Friday morning was spent in united prayer. It was not easy for an eighteen-year-old to be quiet and patiently wait on God. The lessons learned were more important than mere book learning."

Six months after Ernest entered training, the mission found it necessary to close the school. What now? Thompson was sure God had called him and was delighted when the mission leader suggested he go right into the work in Ireland.

For the next three years Ernest labored with others in the Gospel throughout the rural areas. Thompson speaks warmly of that practical missionary experience: "They were the most important years of my preparation. I discovered God could use me and I learned to depend on the Holy Spirit."

Satan has other weapons besides doubt to unleash

upon front-line Christian workers. Here was Thompson, dedicated, a hard worker, and newly on fire with the life of God. How could he be sidetracked? Would a romance do it? If he could not be trapped into falling for the wrong woman, perhaps he could be tempted to put the right girl before God in his life.

Mission boards perforce are marriage counselors. They cannot afford to finance wobbly partnerships. The missionary's home life can defeat the spread of the Gospel and hamper the growth of believers. How many missionary casualties result from explosions at the breakfast table?

To ensure that both members of a household were equally equipped and dedicated for the missionary task, the China Inland Mission long held to a stern ruling. All single people who were accepted by the mission must serve two years in China before they would be permitted to marry. Thus they would have time to learn the language, to get used to the rice and the lice, and to back out, if need be, without pulling another missionary out with them.

The ruling hit R.E. hard. Thompson proposed to Ella Mulligan one summer vacation in Ireland. Brighter-eyed lass never said "Yes" to more eager Irish lad. She knew her "Yes" meant China. R.E. had finished two years of preparatory study in London and was due to sail soon. With joyful pride he announced his engagement to the mission leaders.

Their advice stunned him: "Proceed to China. Let the young lady finish her education here—two years of normal school and one year at the C.I.M. headquarters—and then she may go to China."

Three years! How can you ask a young couple in love to wait three years? Thompson wrestled with it alone in his room before writing to Ella. Should they marry and apply to another mission? No, he knew God had directed him to the C.I.M. But three years of eating his heart out on the other side of the world from his sweetheart!

After a torment of indecision, Thompson received a sense of divine peace and resolution. Since he had joined the China Inland Mission in obedience to God, he would accept its direction as the leading of the Lord. Ella received the hard news with a gentle acquiescence that made R.E. all the more certain she was the girl for him.

When his soft-voiced, bright-eyed fiancee arrived in Shanghai three years later, Thompson was there to meet her. But not to marry her. Not yet. She had to serve two years as a single woman, learning the language and getting oriented. Again the Lord gave them grace to accept the ruling of the mission He had called them to serve.

How many times in their China ministry God used them because they had learned well the disciplines of obedience and separation!

Initiative . . . genuine spiritual life . . . obedience —with these qualities and his native Irish humor, Thompson needed just one thing more—a loving sympathy which became his as the golden result of fiery trials.

Yes, R. E. Thompson is a man I listened to in China and a counselor I will send our mission candidates to today.

CHAPTER 18

The Ordinary Man

"I am afraid there is not too much of the significant about my life or ministry."

This sentence from Bobby Bowman's letter caught me. It was exactly what I was looking for. The story of an ordinary man with an ordinary experience. This would give the ordinary person a handle—something to which he could relate. So I did a little reminiscing and rewarding research.

I discovered that Bob Bowman's ministry has been honored of God to a rather significant degree. It reads like I imagine the twenty-ninth and thirtieth chapters of the Book of Acts might read.

In 1946, I first visited the Far East Broadcasting Company compound in Manila—twelve acres of rice paddies and snake-infested jungle destined to be cleared for the first wooden transmitter building. Now quonset huts and cement buildings mushroom among eighteen different antenna systems topped by a three-hundred-foot medium wave antenna tower.

Today F.E.B.C. operates five complete program services from Manila. There are two Philippine services as well as the English service, and two overseas services. These programs are broadcast simultaneously over fourteen different frequencies, making a total of sixty-eight program hours on the air each day.

ROBERT H. BOWMAN
Missionary to the Philippines
Founder and President of the
Far East Broadcasting Company

The rapid growth of F.E.B.C. saw the establishment of thirteen Philippine stations. Reaching north the organization built three stations on the once devastated island of Okinawa. For seventeen hours a day, KSDX voices the Words of Life in Japanese to the native fishermen of the island. At Naha station, KSAB provides programs in English for the thousands of American servicemen stationed there.

The newest station, KSBU, is a hundred-thousand-watt giant with a four-tower antenna. Anchored to the coral at the water's edge, KSBU looks out over 350 miles of the East China Sea and beams the message of redemption into Red China.

F.E.B.C.'s seventeenth international broadcasting station is situated in San Francisco Bay at Belmont, California. KGEI's fifty thousand watts were once used by the Office of War Information. Today the "Voice of Friendship" sounds spiritual hope southward to Mexico and on to the frigid tip of Argentina.

The Far East Broadcasting Company relies on the miracle-working God Who built and sustains it. The project began in 1945 with three young men pooling their meager resources. Bill Roberts, a tender-hearted California pastor, was experienced in radio evangelism. Bob Bowman was baritone soloist for the "Haven of Rest" broadcast. John Broger had just given up a $1,400-a-month job to devote himself to God's service. Broger, Roberts, and Bowman had one thing in common—their concern for those in the Orient who had never heard of Christ's saving love.

Today, from Tokyo to Bombay, from Peking to Djakarta, covering Asia and all of Latin America, the Far East Broadcasting Company sends out the message of eternal life through Jesus Christ. Over seventeen powerful transmitters in thirty-six languages of Asia and four of Latin America, F.E.B.C. broadcasts cover an area where two billion, three hundred million people live.

This is significant . . . this is big . . . this is a miracle. I have mentioned three men, but I want you to take a good look at the man who humbly wrote,

"I am afraid there is not too much of the significant about my life."

Bob Bowman is one of those rare Californians actually born there. His mother, a woman of spiritual depth and Christian warmth, was a living example to young Bobby, his sister and three brothers. Her consistent Christian life brought deepening conviction to the heart of Bob's father. About the time Bob reached his fifteenth birthday, Mr. Bowman was converted. This new Christian dimension strengthened the home and family life.

But Bob could not be a Christian simply because his parents were. One evening in a church in Inglewood, California, Bob acknowledged that he was a sinner and took Jesus Christ as his personal Savior.

High school days were filled with the usual sub-Christian experience of the average teen-ager. Bob's spiritual thermometer moved from cold to lukewarm to hot and back to lukewarm. But as he reached his senior year his love for the Lord Jesus Christ deepened and his desire to know more of the Word of God intensified.

Not knowing God's will for his life but sensing this hunger and need, he determined to go to Bible school. During Bible school days missions became a very important part of his learning. Eventually the Lord began to deal with him about the regions beyond where Christ was not known.

Bob admits to months of struggle, and of that period says, "I fought the Lord and His will as I contemplated the possibility of God calling me to the mission field. Eventually I gave up the struggle and He won. I yielded my heart completely to Him. Now I prayed most earnestly that God would show me the field of His choice for me and wondered if it might be China or Africa. There were many hours and days of prayer on behalf of missions during this time.

"The reading of two important books influenced me greatly. Hudson Taylor's life shook me. I wanted to be that kind of a man. The life of Henry Martin of India also left its deep impression upon me. He was the man who uttered those never-to-be-forgotten words as he landed on India's shores, 'Now let me burn out for God.' The fact that he did burn out for God in six brief years, yet accomplished so much, assured me that God would hear my cry if my commitment were as real as his."

Bob was not only influenced by the lives of Taylor and Martin. He was captivated by the commitment and beauty of an art student. Eleanor was Bob's match then and has been during the three decades of their life together in meeting any sacrifice involved in carrying out God's purpose for their lives and ministry.

All during Bible college God had His hand upon Bob, leading him, training him, teaching him. In Bob's second year the opportunity opened for him to sing with the "Haven of Rest" quartet. For twelve years he carried on this work. Bob's appealing baritone voice was soon known to millions, and Bob became convinced of the value of radio in reaching masses of people for Christ. Bob took to radio like a duck to water. He liked it and it liked him.

"The opportunity and the very fruitfulness of the 'Haven of Rest' ministry could have kept me from God's future plan," Bob confesses.

It would have been easy to talk himself into believing that this was the will of God for the rest of his life. The First Mate on the "Haven of Rest" broadcast had groomed Bob to take his place before the microphone and Bob had many occasions to do so. He was a natural for the job.

Was not God's blessing upon his ministry at home sufficient evidence that this was the will of God? It all seemed so logical. But the will of God supersedes plain logic. Although in a quiet way Bowman puts everyone at ease, he is not the kind of man who takes the line of least resistance. He would know God's will and, knowing it, would obey, irrespective of the cost.

Bob admits that the struggle that culminated in the birth of the F.E.B.C. was a real one.

"You are counting. You are serving. Stay where you are. You have a wife and family to support. Don't upset the applecart. Stay where you are ... stay where you are. You are needed here. Stay where you are. Here you have a regular salary. What will happen to your family if you leave it? Doesn't the Scripture warn that 'anyone who won't care for his . . . own family, has no right to say he is a Christian. Such a person is worse than the heathen' (1 Timothy 5:8, *Living Letters*)? Then stay where you are."

A hundred arguments pounded on his brain. Bob could not deny the logic of the disquieting voice. But once he was convinced he must move on to be in the will of God, *he moved*.

This was not Bob's only struggle. In everyone's life the natural man always wants his way. Victory is only won through waiting upon the Lord in daily communion, living in the Word, and obeying what God says. Bob's greatest struggle was in relation to his own personal life—those inward secret things that demand obedience to the Holy Spirit.

This man, so overflowing with Christian graciousness, confesses, "For obedience to Christ in these areas my heart continually cries out that I might be more like Him and a better instrument for His glory. Eagerness to start the race, to jump ahead, to move like a young colt, must be checked by obedience. When the battle gets too hot and the temptation to retreat or to relax pushes heavy, obedience to the call of Christ to move forward, to press on with the task, to never give up, is imperative.

"When temptation comes to seek an easier life, I am called back by the thought of Paul who said, 'Woe is me if I preach not the Gospel.' "

Bob Bowman is an ordinary man but *an obedient man*. Through this ordinary but obedient man and his team, today millions who otherwise might never hear are hearing the Gospel.

If he were ordinary and disobedient to the will of God, chances are we would have never heard of him. Get the message?

CHAPTER 19

How Bill Got Hooked

Bill McKee a *missionary?* Never! He had seen too many of those "birds" and they all had dull feathers. Bill wanted no part in the "missionary barrel life"— he was too fond of flashy clothes.

"Sure, it is great to be a Christian but don't be a fanatic, Bill," he would say to himself.

But the great Fisherman was after him and Bill got hooked at a Youth for Christ rally. There he promised Jesus Christ he would *"be anything, go anywhere."* That should have settled it but Bill admits he traveled a bumpy road ahead.

The more missionaries Bill saw and heard, the more he tried to convince himself (and God) that maybe some other occupation should be his mission field. In other words, he was not at all impressed by mission representatives and their discourses on sacrifice and deprivation. He, like some others, began saying, "Here am I, Lord. Send somebody else." But God never let Bill forget his promise to "be anything, go anywhere" for Christ.

During Bill's turbulent teen years the ministry of Dr. H. H. Savage and the constant missionary emphasis of the church was making its impact. The faithfulness of a mother who prayed the Lord of the harvest

BILL McKEE
Missionary to the Philippines
and Missionary-at-Large
with Overseas Crusades

to thrust out laborers—and put her son at the top of the list—bombarded heaven. And the loving concern of Mr. and Mrs. Ralph Pardee, who let the teens tear up their home every Friday night for the chance to tell them God's way was best, slowly pierced Bill's armor.

But Bill confesses, "After high school I drifted for a year without any clear direction." Direction finally came, but not in the form of a brick from the blue or an emotional experience. It came through a guy named Tom Ainge. He saw Bill's life starting to settle into a foxhole of complacency so he asked him to take a little trip with him. The trip ended on the campus of a Christian college—where Bill later enrolled.

"You're not spiritual!"

"You're square!"

These statements represented the attitudes of the two distinctly different groups Bill met in college. The one was made up of the *"no makeup—did you have your devotions this morning?—I'm on the way to the mission field"* group. The other represented the fun-loving group *that seemed to be majoring in foolishness and extra-curricular activities.* Bill became a leader of the latter group and the conflict with what he had promised God and what he was doing raged anew inside him.

But once again God used people. Veteran missionary Dr. Harry Stam, Dr. J. Edwin Hartill and Professor Bill Berntsen were men who looked deep and saw under the facade of fun and seeming disinterest a heart that longed for God and His perfect plan. They helped to hold Bill steady.

Then Bill met a missionary who shattered his image of what a missionary was supposed to look and sound like. The light that entered turned on his life! The light "went on" at the Friday chapel hour. On Friday the speaker was usually a missionary. Bill describes his Friday routine:

"We would sing 'Far, far away in heathen darkness dwelling,' take one look at the missionary and then study for our next class. But this Friday was not routine. This guy was sharp and he was dressed in style. He had an eager 'I'm in the best business in the world' manner about him. I listened! I didn't hear the word 'sacrifice' once. He didn't tell any sad stories or talk about his problems. He talked about miracles—and we knew he was talking from experience. He talked about the positive privilege of being an ambassador for Christ. Within me things were falling into place. I could hardly wait to get up there to talk to him and find out what mission he was with. He was from Overseas Crusades—a young mission with fresh, vibrant ideas on how to stimulate and mobilize the Church to evangelism. Here am I, Lord, send *me*. Yes, Lord, 'be anything, go anywhere.' "

In college Bill fell in love with a lovely brunette. The discussions Sharon and Bill had about the future resulted in some confusion regarding her part in missionary work. She had not been "called." But Bill thought he had. What is a call? They had heard missionaries use the word so much but never define it. Was it a Damascus Road experience? An emotion-charged missionary meeting? A voice in the night? What? They only knew she hadn't been called and although Bill *knew* he was going to the mission field he wasn't *sure* he had been called either. Commanded—yes! But called???

Following their marriage they continued to pray and talk and question. They were told to pray about it and wait. They were told to "hang on," to let go, to listen for the "call." Finally, on a retreat they found the answer as a pastor talked about God's will. He said, "Some of you girls are terribly concerned because you don't feel called to do what your husband feels he must do." Bill and Sharon tensed and waited. The pastor continued, "First, has God ordained your marriage?" Yes! They almost said it out loud. "Are you willing to go with him?" Yes, again. "Then go! Be his helpmeet. You are both one—what God has told the husband is for the wife too." Bill and Sharon had found their answer and they had a hard time seeing or speaking as the peace of God flooded their hearts.

They still had questions. What mission? Where should they go? To a certain people? To a particular geographic location? More questions, more decisions. But questions and decisions are good for one. Bill says, "As I look back I see that all this led to more dependence upon God and His promise, 'Trust in the Lord with all thine heart; and lean not unto thine own understanding. In all thy ways acknowledge him, and he shall direct thy paths' (Proverbs 3:5, 6). These crossroads or seeming dead ends cast us totally on Him and taught us invaluable lessons. Ours to trust—His to see if we would."

But they couldn't just sit around. This, Bill and Sharon had learned. Sharon wrote a dozen mission boards—some denominational, some interdenominational, some specialist groups. "We told them our qualifications, asked them to advise us concerning their requirements—educational and otherwise—and asked them to pray for us," Sharon recalls. "Some never answered. Others were vague. But as the replies came we prayed."

And God sent a man! God saw that Bill and Sharon meant business. They were not going to settle down saying they were willing or had tried and let it go at that. Bill picks up the story, "As Dr. Dick Hillis spoke our hearts burned within us. Oh, yes, Dick just happened to be—and still is—the General Director of that young mission we mentioned earlier, Overseas Crusades. Wasn't that a coincidence? No, it was not! We had made some moves—right or wrong we had moved—motivated by the desire to know and do His will. Now *He* was moving—to indicate that will."

"We had Dr. Hillis in our home and really fired the questions. He had the answers. Some of them were not as neat and rosy as we may have liked, but he was honest and gave us the whole picture. Again we prayed and God's deep peace—which became a sort of spiritual barometer of His will for us—began to seep into our souls. So we moved again and applied to Overseas Crusades. We had no special direction as far as place or people, but simply trusted the discernment of godly men in the mission. This too proved right, and the barometer of His peace has not fallen once."

For nine years Bill and Sharon served in the Orient. Now their field is "the world." And Bill says, "It's phenomenal! this being in the will of God. It is life—*life with meaning!*"

CHAPTER 20

Breaking the Sound Barrier

I was "called" before I was "saved." Yes, our terms—"called," "saved," "consecrated," committed"—are seldom big enough to fit our experiences. And our God is so much bigger than our terms that He can turn them around to suit His own purposes.

The first inclination God wanted me in China came when I was thirteen years old and a freshman in high school.

Our little Methodist church in the great Northwest set aside one week each year for evangelistic meetings. My folks attended every meeting. To please them, Don, my twin brother, Harry, our older brother, and I went along. Going got us out of tiring homework and gave us an opportunity to see "the gang."

In 1926, Dr. George Bennard, the author of "The Old Rugged Cross," was invited as the evangelist. I confess I have no idea of the content of any of Dr. Bennard's messages, least of all what he said on that Thursday evening. He did not speak on missions but when he gave an invitation to accept Christ, I came under such conviction that God wanted me to be a missionary to China that I rushed to the wooden altar rail to tell God I would go.

Long minutes later I stood up and left the altar.

DR. DICK HILLIS
Missionary to China under the
China Inland Mission
Founder and General Director of
Overseas Crusades, Inc.

As I walked out to the Model A Ford, I was aware that China was my destination and God was my Boss.

In the car on the way home I told Mother and Dad of my decision to be a missionary. Their reaction was one of real joy. "We gave you to God before you were born," Mother said.

For a few months I really worked at this new enterprise. But the tide was too strong. Other things were just more interesting—school, the gang, football, and the excitement of staying free to run my own life. As the months passed I discovered that it takes more than a trip to the altar to make a missionary. Becoming a missionary seemed unreal and far away. I tried . . . I failed . . . so why not forget the whole thing?

I soon eased back into the main current of high school life. Now and then I experienced a twinge of conscience. I had made a vow to God and gone back on it. But so, I told myself, had millions of other people.

Strangely, I found it easier to cloud God from my thoughts than to wipe China from the horizon. The great cosmopolitan city of Shanghai intrigued me. Its multiracial populace promised more opportunity and excitement than any city in the world.

I dreamed: When high school days were over I would leave home, cross the Pacific, and drop out of sight amidst Shanghai's colorful multitudes. Ten years later I would re-appear, a bright star out of the East, to dazzle my parents with the fame and fortune I gained in Cathay.

Wild dream! Of course! But God condescendingly mixed a large portion of His plan with a little of my plot. Before my story ends you will see how I went to China with *Him* rather than alone.

My part was to become restless and go to California. Although I loved my parents, I rebelled against a little town, little church, and little people. I would go to a big city like Los Angeles and be big with it.

God's part was to get me from Los Angeles to Shanghai. Now between Los Angeles and Shanghai there is a lot of water, and between my dream and God's design were two hundred and eight weeks and twice that many miracles.

The first big miracle took place on Sunday evening in the Church of the Open Door in Los Angeles. My twin brother had entered Biola to prepare for the ministry. To be with him I also entered Biola, so we were both in church that night.

At the altar the Holy Spirit brought to my heart the peace that only comes with the assurance of salvation. Now I grew excited about discovering God's will for my life. I determined to find it . . . and to obey. God's first gracious move was to teach me something about a walk of reliance upon Him.

"Faith without works is dead," and work I did. To me each job came as an answer to prayer. On the day I was about to go without eating, a restaurant called for a bus boy. Or a lady gave me work waxing her kitchen floor or pruning her fruit trees. God proved faithful.

The teaching at Biola was not simply academic. Men of God presented the Scripture in such a way that it took on flesh and blood. I felt that I must be a missionary *now,* not at some future date. There were plenty of opportunities, and I took many of them: Sunday school classes . . . street meetings . . . jail services . . . rescue missions . . . Gospel teams . . . and preaching assignments.

I could not take in the rich truths of the Gospel without giving them out. I would bust. I was getting more than lessons and theology. I was meeting a *Person* face to face and *meeting Him* impels one to introduce Him to others.

And what happened to the China dream? I was too busy to think about China. After all, I was a missionary of sorts in Los Angeles.

Honesty forces me to admit that the sight of a lovely girl also played a part in making a foreign land less attractive. I first saw her at a Biola banquet.

"Did you notice that attractive, smiling brunette sitting across from you, Ken?" I asked.

"Notice her? You guess I did, Dick. Couldn't take my eyes off her."

After a little spy work Ken reported, "Her name is Margaret Humphrey. She is eighteen, a serious Christian, and a good student. And as of this moment she is not going with anyone."

Whether she had a boy friend in her home town of Yakima, Ken did not know.

140

I had gone with girls. Some I liked. Some I didn't. From that night on I could not get Margaret off my mind. I watched her in class. I used any excuse to get close enough to talk with her. As I sat in my squeaky study chair, her pretty face would flash before me and I would dream.

I managed one date—tennis together—before she started going with a friend. Now my lonely avenue became prayer. I wrote her name on the top of my prayer list and asked God to give her to me. She became my one concern. She was more important than China or the man across the street . . . more important than anything.

Then God used a class on Romans to force me to square up to the fact that I must be concerned about the man across the sea as well as the one across the street.

As the class moved through the first three chapters of Romans, the Holy Spirit so illuminated the truths that it was like coming out of the long night of an Alaskan winter. First, the awfulness of millions being lost without Christ set up such a mental conflict that for a time I questioned that "God is love."

But as I struggled and studied, the Holy Spirit took me to the Hill of the Skull. There I realized that the love and holiness, the wrath and justice of God are simply part of His perfect immutable character. Does Calvary speak of unsurpassed love or of righteous wrath? Both! Righteous wrath toward sin and abiding love toward the sinner.

"He that spared not his own Son" (Romans 8: 32) forever satisfied me that God loves lost mankind. Now I heard the cry of the millions across the sea. They suddenly became my personal responsibility. I could not—and do not think I really wanted to—avoid those searching questions Paul asks in the Book of Romans:

"But how shall they ask Him to save them unless they believe in Him? And how can they believe in Him if they have never heard about Him? And how can they hear about Him unless someone tells them? And how will anyone go and tell them unless someone sends him?" (Romans 10:14, 15, *Living Letters*).

But was it China or was that simply a boyhood dream? I set about to find out. Each week I went to the library to study the people and customs of a different country.

I bought a National Geographic World Map and in alphabetic order prayed for different countries each day.

At the sacrifice of other things I made it a point to hear every missionary speaker possible.

Every missionary biography I could get my hands on I read.

I sought out missionaries to question them about their work and the needs on their fields.

In order to understand "faith missions" I asked three to put me on their mailing lists.

The more I searched the more intense grew the conviction that God did want me to serve Him in China. But this seemed so insane. God knew, better than I, that language was by far my poorest subject. Even with a sympathetic teacher and some special tutoring, the best grade I could pull in Spanish was a "D." And my conscience told me I hardly deserved it. It just did not make sense. It was so illogical that I should go to China to a people whose language is one of the most difficult in the world.

Another thing did not make sense. The Chinese language is tonal and I am only one grade point above tone deaf. One should be musical to speak Chinese and artistic to write its characters. I am neither musical nor artistic and, to add insult to injury, I possess a good forgetter.

How could I be expected to retain thousands of Chinese characters—characters that to the novice look like they were written by a drunken chicken?

"No," I said to myself a hundred times, "it just isn't logical. God does not want me in China. What if I went, flunked the language, and came home a missionary casualty? Such action certainly would not bring glory to God."

As I struggled with this problem, I was reading through the Book of Exodus. Assuring God and attempting to reassure myself that if it were not for the "language problem" I would gladly go, I opened the Word of God. It was Wednesday and my reading was in the fourth chapter. In verse ten I was struck with the excuses Moses made for not obeying Jehovah's orders:

"I am not eloquent," he complained.

"I am slow of speech, and of a slow tongue."

My excuses were not too different from the ones Moses made in his encounter with God. I felt rebuked.

"And the Lord said unto him, Who hath made man's mouth? . . . have not I the Lord?" (Exodus 4:11).

In the same way that God answered Moses' arguments some three thousand years ago, He now talked to me, "Dick, who made your mouth? Have not I the Lord?"

Thoughts raced through my mind with such rapidity they tumbled over one another. In obedience situations that seem illogical become reasonable. Does not acceptance of God's will guarantee success? Will He not enable me to do whatever He appoints me to do? Does not the treasure in an "earthen vessel" bring more glory to the treasure? Is it not like God to give you the task and even send you to the place that is hardest for you so that His grace can be more fully manifest through you?

Like a man whose cataracts were removed so he could see again I saw that God had a right to send me any place and that I had a right to believe He would see me through. God stops Moses' arguments with a command to obey and a promise to enable, "Now therefore go, and I will be with thy mouth, and teach thee what thou shalt say" (Exodus 4:12).

That morning God gave me the same command and assured me with the same promise. My response was not sensational but it was sincere, "I will go, Lord, and trust You to teach my mouth the Chinese language."

Beside the verse I wrote, "God's *promise* to me for China." *God kept His promise* and after a few months of struggle with strange Chinese words, I broke the sound barrier.

And what about that girl? Here also God was faithful. Seven years after I first laid my eyes on her lovely face, we stood together in the city of

Hankow, China, and repeated our sacred marriage vows.

God never withholds what is best for you if you are in His will. Why should He? And why should you delay in discovering His will?

When you pray, "May Your will be done here on earth, just as it is in heaven" (Matthew 6:10, *Living Gospels*), you are asking God to work out His will in your life on earth as perfectly as the angels in heaven perform His will.

Have you been mumbling words or do you mean it? The fruit of "*my will*" is frustration and failure. The fruit of "*Thy will*" is life—exciting, fulfilling, and meaningful.

And what must one do? Sincerely and honestly pray, "May Your will be done," and then put muscles to your words. And what do I mean by muscles?

The men and women in this book believed God wanted them in foreign service. Their belief determined their actions.

Did they face problems? Plenty of them.

Were they ever perplexed? You know they were.

Did discouragement threaten them? They are human.

Were obstacles thrown in their paths? Mountains of them.

These common heroes were led to climb. Though sometimes faced by winds of adversity and storms of protest, they overcame problems and, in the Name of the One Who told them to climb, conquered. They learned that to climb one must add

to vision, determination;

to determination, preparation;

to preparation, perseverance;

to perseverance, patience;

to patience, plodding.

They discovered that decision is five percent and follow-through is ninety-five percent. Their stories have been told to encourage you to climb. Your problems are not too different from the ones they faced.

They climbed and conquered.

You, too, were born to climb!